Without Bombast And Blunders

An Executive's Guide to Effective Writing

FRANCES D. NACZI

FARNSWORTH PUBLISHING COMPANY, INC.
Rockville Centre, New York 11570

© 1980. Frances D. Naczi.
All rights reserved.
First printing, September 1980.
Published by Farnsworth Publishing Co., Inc.
Rockville Centre, New York 11570.
Library of Congress Catalog Card No. 80-17857.
ISBN 0-87863-007-4.
Manufactured in the United States of America.

Library of Congress Cataloging in Publication Data

Naczi, Frances D.
    Without bombast and blunders.

        Bibliography: p.
        1. English language—Business English.   2. English
language—Rhetoric.   I. Title.
PE1115.N3   808'.066651021   80-17857
ISBN 0-87863-007-4

In Memory of My Father

Francis P. Daily

and for My Family, with Love

ACKNOWLEDGMENTS

My Deepest Thanks to

The Reverend Stephen P. Breen, Ph.D.
For Special Help and Encouragement

Phillip J. Wingate, Ph.D.
Gracious Contributor

Marjorie Spector
Mentor and Editor

Foreword

Frances D. Naczi, who wrote this book, has a better opinion of men, in general, and businessmen and women in particular, than either Charles Francis Adams or H.L. Mencken.

Adams, the son of John Quincy Adams and the grandson of John Adams, said that while he had associated with many of the nation's top business executives all his life, he never heard one of them say anything worth hearing.

Mencken was somewhat kinder but declared that "A man's womenfolk, whatever their outward show of respect for his merit and authority, always regard him secretly as an ass and with something akin to pity. His most gaudy sayings and doings seldom deceive them, they see the actual man within and know him for a shallow and pathetic fellow."

Mrs. Naczi believes that all men are by no means shallow and pathetic and that men and women in the business world often say something worth listening to, but she does wish they would learn to say it—and write it—more gracefully.

If they read this book carefully, they probably will learn to communicate effectively—and without bombast and blunder.

Phillip J. Wingate, Ph.D.
Vice-President and General Manager (ret.)
E.I. duPont de Nemours, Inc.

When you've got a thing to say,

Say it! Don't take half a day....

Life is short—a fleeting vapor—

Don't you fill the whole blamed paper

With a tale which, at a pinch,

Could be cornered in an inch!

Boil her down until she simmers,

Polish her until she glimmers.

Joel Chandler Harris

Advice to Writers

TABLE OF CONTENTS

FOREWORD

1. THE EXECUTIVE EPISTLE   7
   An Overview

2. GETTING IT ALL TOGETHER   19
   Where and When To Go,
   How To Get There and Why

3. MOVING RIGHT ALONG   31
   Anatomy of an Opener and a Close

4. SOLECISM AND OTHER SINS   49
   How Words Work For or Against You

5. FROM IDEA TO EXPRESSION   71
   With Clarity, Unity and Coherence

6. THE ART OF DE-SEXING   83
   Devices To Avoid Discrimination

7. THE GREAT DICTATORS   99
   And Those Who Aren't

8. MEMOS AND OTHER MISERIES   111
   Breaking the Bafflegab Barrier

9. EACH TO ITS OWN   133
   For Every Purpose a Letter

10. THE BOTTOM LINE   149
    Cost and Effect of Communication

DECALOGUE   163
EPILOGUE   165
BIBLIOGRAPHY   169
   Recommended Reading/Dictionaries/Subject
   Dictionaries

INDEX   173

It is difficult enough to write a successful letter while the writer's frame of mind is happiest, but when the writer is cranky or sour on the world, one letter may cost thousands of dollars.

1.

The Executive Epistle

An Overview

Executive suites throughout corporate America have turned into paper mills grinding out billions of top-level communications, many of which are not worth the impressive letterheads on which they are written.

Too many business messages fail as effective communication tools. *Nation's Business* reports on studies that state, "At least half of all written messages are misunderstood or misinterpreted somewhere down the line."

Otherwise-learned persons can and do write bad letters. The same mistakes are made over and over, for the same reasons. Why?

The answer is to be found somewhere among the loose cogs of well-oiled corporate machinery. Too little concern is shown for streams of valueless written communications. As the high cost of letters, memos and reports grows higher, there is a growing admission that miscalculation of the value of effective business writing is a gross and common error.

When the real effects of poorly presented information were balanced against the real costs by a few astute administrators, the picture began to change.

One-third of the country's top corporations conduct successful training programs for thousands of junior executives (and those who want to be). Communication seminars and mail order courses are big business. Top officials in every area of business, industry and government are taking greater interest in *what* is written and *how* it is written in their own shops.

Basically, this book is designed for all the concerned, but busy executives who want to push through old barriers of bombast and blunder to new levels of clarity by easily absorbing the concept and simple techniques of modern business writing.

Here are suggestions to learn or re-learn the most important elements of business writing. For those who may have been bypassed by a few changes during the years, we offer guidelines for updating language usage and discarding old habits.

Nevertheless, not every book or clinic in itself can motivate a person to be a good business writer. The need to work smarter, not harder, will make it happen.

Simplification is smart. Already, correction and clarification of outmoded businessese and legalese in employee benefit plans, warranties, financial statements, consumer credit forms, insurance policies, etc., are dealing a deathblow to bombastic language. The goal is to establish a nationwide single standard of understandability.

The Costs of Business Writing

The effect business writing has on "The Bottom Line" (Chapter 10), where it hurts or helps the most, should be of greater concern to the cost-conscious (and isn't everybody?).

According to a 1979 study by the Dartnell Institute of Business Research, the real cost of a fifteen-cent business letter averages $5.59 and is steadily rising. Yet rarely does consideration of correspondence as one of the major budget-eaters go beyond itemizing the cost of feeding the postage meter.

Although the stamp is the smallest part of a letter, there is no certainty about how much its cost will jump by 1981. The Postal Service is planning digitless stamps (to provide elasticity in rates) and a change from the current five-digit to a nine-digit ZIP code system in 1981. It is also moving in several fascinating directions in the electronic message delivery area.

"When we increase postage rates, we're passing on higher costs to users, not taxpayers," said Postmaster General William Bolger. "And the biggest users are businesses, generating 94 percent of the mail. Only 6 percent is personal correspondence."

Other factors to be discussed more fully in Chapter 10, include the increased cost of stationery and other supplies forecast to rise 62 percent from now through 1985. Further, the expenditures for office support staffs are reaching staggering proportions and the value of your executive time has also escalated.

As we calculate and balance costs against gains, one conclusion is obvious: both talent and materials must be used more wisely. The proliferation of ineffective written communications is simply inefficient.

Say the Most With the Least

How does one control the volume of paper flow in busy offices? Among the methods proposed, saying the most with the least cuts the quantity and improves the quality. Most files are cluttered with two-page letters that could have said it all in one page if the writers had known how to get the messages to you in a concise, complete and correct form.

Are you inundated with reports that are ten pages longer than they should be so they will appear to be complete and thorough? This is more of a bureaucratic process than a corporate practice. Nevertheless, word-watchers agree more agencies are promulgating the use of simple language albeit too abundantly.

For instance, the former Department of Health, Education and Welfare's "Operation Common Sense" introduced a five-year program in 1978 to purge bureaucratic bafflegab from 6,000 pages of regulations. Joseph A. Califano, then HEW Secretary, issued a directive for streamlining the paperwork. His plan covered 36 pages! Also, HUD's simplified land-sales regulations ended up 20 percent longer than the unsimplified version.

A new group, Plain Talk, Inc., fights gobbledygook in government and business. It will give a "Golden Shovel" award to the worst offenders.

Morale and Meaning

Cost factors of business writing can be measured in more ways than dollars and cents. Any depletion of morale and efficiency caused by a poor quality of communication can be serious, as any good manager knows. How can words be used more effectively to prevent this loss or breakdown in communication?

Take a look. Where's a large part of your workload? Does that pile of letters, memos, reports, proposals, etc., challenge your expertise in verbal expression and time management? Do the daily problems of paperwork contribute to executive stress and strain? Here are guidelines to relieve the strain and upgrade your company's rapport with its employees and the public at the same time.

For instance, gone are the days of long, complex and confusing letters that seem to have been prepared by a programmed robot instead of a real person. Every modern manager realizes that all communication efforts involve other human beings, directly or indirectly.

One of the greater mysteries is why so many business and professional persons who are noted for expert problem-solving and other administrative abilities give business writing second best or no consideration.

Employees, too, expect the best from the top. Thus, the language of in-house communiques has become more exact. Errors and cloudy meanings in "Memos and Other Miseries" (Chapter 8) stimulate comments from those who are seldom exasperated by their own ineptness.

Edmund Burke wrote: "A very great part of the mischiefs that vex this world arises from words." You know this prevails in the business world. Too many ineptly written in-house messages are misunderstood and misinterpreted. They often spread unfounded rumors, elicit blasé attitudes and weaken when they should strengthen employee motivation.

"Memos and Other Miseries" (Chapter 8) should increase your knowledge of the preparation of various forms of business writing. How do they differ? What are the most important elements of these "power tools" that can make decisions, spur actions, or convey information?

Expressing Yourself—Clearly

Much of the problem stems from time-worn habits that block the expression of direct and natural thoughts. "From Idea to Expression" (Chapter 5) leads you along the route to greater clarity, unity and coherence. How do you project a tone and a style that keeps the reader in mind? What are the disadvantages of writing as you speak? What sounds clear to you may be read unclear.

Yes, bafflegab is out of style. This is why it becomes necessary to explore the forms and reasons for Standard English with it preciseness of language.

For this reason, you are invited to refresh your memory of "Solecism and Other Sins" (Chapter 4) and repent, if necessary. Here is a valuable discussion of misused, overused, outmoded and overblown words and phrases commonly found in corporate correspondence.

This chapter, however, is not a lengthy treatise on grammatical rules. That is not to say that grammar is unimportant; its loose practice often smudges executive images and obfuscates messages. At your level, however, the most prevalent errors are correctable largely by common sense, careful attention to inadvertent blunders, and a more thorough attention to basic rules.

The ability to manipulate words will be your major asset. Using the language skillfully will help you say what you mean, simply and effectively. Sentence construction and work usage can make or break comprehension, weaken or strengthen, or set the tone for better or worse results.

Chapter 4 brings into focus the way words can work for you. It proposes the elimination of high-sounding phrases, "stringy" sentences, and excess verbiage that cause confusion and boredom—yours and the reader's.

Here's how to recognize and use the energy of words to make limp and flabby messages come alive. Do you lapse into the passive voice thoughtlessly? How can you write less and with more meaning? Do you ramble needlessly while searching for words and phrases to express an idea? Can you confine one thought to a sentence and sustain continuity?

How can the techniques of proper word usage and construction be applied to "De-Sexing the Language" (Chapter 6)? Here is a discussion of a relatively new writing art form that can no longer be avoided. Corporations are now tied to a national movement that would avoid discrimination between the sexes. Accordingly, a clearer view of the ways language can be used to give both men and women fair treatment is needed.

Dictating Do's and Don'ts

The challenge to change well-worn habits seeps into every aspect of business writing. For instance, what of the mannerisms that flow too freely during a dictation session? Are your secretaries in an almost constant state of bewilderment? How much time do you spend painfully extracting the right words and reliable information from your mind in the midst of a dictation session? When you have read what has been wrought, do you recognize the language as your own? Could this oratory have sprung from one who is usually controlled, conservative and somewhat diffident? Conversely, are you the vociferous executive who sometimes freezes into a silent state when faced with a dictaphone, tape recorder, or a new secretary?

"The Great Dictators" (Chapter 7) offers remedial action to the various types of dictators including The Rambler, The Erratic, The Mumbler, The Analyst, The Rapid-Fire Dictator and the ordinary business person who simply wants dictation to go more smoothly and produce results worthy of the effort.

Special Letters

"Each To Its Own" (Chapter 9) reviews the various approaches and methods of writing letters for specific purposes. As you know, there is a format for each type of letter; a technique to bring desired results. Which one is best for each of your purposes?

If you can write a good sales letter, for instance, other writing tasks will be less formidable. Everyone lives by selling something! Every letter, in a sense, is a sales letter when it projects the best picture of you, your company and its products and services. With the reader in mind as the basic rule, the components and concepts of each type of letter can teach us something applicable to all communication.

Good letters, designed to meet important needs, also can justify the high cost of office automation. Many computer and form letters, although essential to meet heavy demands in large companies, cannot be regarded as infallible by virtue of electronic output. The input is still essential; words come first. It is unlikely that the creators of word processors, electronic mail systems, facsimile, microform and other technological wonders will produce equipment—in our lifetimes—to replace the human brain. Nevertheless, they are changing the way we do business.

Plunge In—Slowly

"Getting It All Together" (Chapter 2) is the first step. Most executives are eminently suited to this mental process. They know the basic principles of good business writing are no more mysterious than other management qualifications. Both evolve from desire, honesty, knowledge and information.

Whenever you have implemented an idea, made a decision, proposed an action, approved a major purchase, there has been pre-planning—if only in the mind. Yet how often have you jumped into writing an important "Executive Epistle" with only a vague notion of a goal and a stereotyped phrase or two as a warm-up exercise?

Where does a letter really begin? How is a clumsy structure avoided? Certainly, it's easier to correct a thought than rewrite a garbled sentence.

What kind of opening attracts attention and compels sufficient interest to read on? How do you bring a message to an effective close that will bring results? The greatest problem in resolving most situations and writing all messages is often how to open and how to close.

A good beginning begets good supportive material and a good ending ties it all together. To get started, simply know where you are going; to end, remember where you've been. Simple techniques, as suggested in "Moving Right Along," (Chapter 3) will lead the way from a structured beginning through an effective ending.

Awareness Is (Almost) All

Don't expect old habits to die suddenly; they fade away with time and effort. This book offers no formula for some mystical change in your communication pattern or style. It does give the busy executive short guides to changes for the better. Above all else, it should create a greater awareness of the need to improve the effectiveness of your company's overall communication efforts. What is good for you is good for your company.

Now you may become more interested in the compilation of new material or the revision of a company style book that defines specific corporate policies relevant to style, form, tone, word usage, etc. Both books would serve as valuable reference materials, especially for secretaries and others who are required to meet your high standards.

There may be a need for an overall improvement in attitude concerning the quality of your corporate communication. Too many believe that some messages are relatively unimportant and not worth their "best shot." This is a common fallacy, a "cop out" at times. Each letter and memo has its effect and its result—good, bad, or indifferent.

While you may enjoy the luxury of assigning others to compose your letters, memos, etc., do you recognize your own responsibility for every word that goes over your signature? This is where your editing skills and thorough knowledge of all that constitutes an effective message comes into play. It is not enough to say "My secretary (or assistant or P.R. Department) writes all my letters. . . ." You sign them and the reader considers them *your* best effort.

Check it out the next time around. Does the quality of work produced by someone else or by a computer properly reflect your own personality and contribute constructively to the corporate image?

Only direct, natural and meaningful messages should be devised for (or by) modern executives. It may be your own know-how that will determine the difference.

This book was written to help every member of a management team to become more confident, to grow in competence and to carry on the game like seasoned players. And most importantly, to give a damn!

There are a thousand thoughts lying within a man he does not know until he takes up his pen to write.
— William Makepeace Thackeray

2.

Getting It All Together

**Where and When To Go,
How To Get There and Why**

Two blind beggars are walking their beats, each carries a sign, a cane, a cup. One of the blind men wears a sign: "I am blind." His cup is empty. The other sign reads: "It is spring and I am blind." His cup is full.

Here is an example of the *effective* and *profitable* use of simple language. Each sign was tailored to the situation, as every good communication should be, yet one had the impact that brought greater results.

An effective "angle" rarely evolves from chance, but from deliberate design.

As you know, the accomplishment of a definite objective begins in the mind. It is this same approach-thinking that spells the difference between success and failure in written communication. Those who think first and write later invariably compose a well-structured message.

Be Prepared

Building the beginning, middle and end of a message that can make or break a business relationship starts in the workshop of your mind when its purpose is first defined.

Regardless of the given problem, the thought process in dealing with it in a letter is much the same as it would be for any other business situation. A plan gives us the opportunity to "get it all together" right at the outset and avoid the hassle of indecisiveness later on because of a lack of preparation.

Before you start to write, think carefully about two related questions: "What precisely do I want to do?" and "How can I best do it?" Answer these questions clearly and you take a giant step toward writing well. By knowing precisely what your purpose is, it becomes easier to realize how particular decisions about choice of material, organization and style will help or hinder that purpose.

Too many letters are written by rote and not by reason. One of the causes is the time element that creates a let's-do-it-and-get-it-over-with attitude. This may result in a hodgepodge of irrelevant, conflicting statements, a midway switch of confusing thoughts and an unfriendly impression you really don't want to give.

The business writer who is generally bored with the whole writing scene, picks up a letter received and, not having read it too thoroughly (if at all), starts dictating or writing "from the top" by telling the reader what he or she already knows—just to get started.

> *Example:* "Your letter dated June 10, 1979 in which you request the cost for a gross of XYZ Widgets that you say you need for use in the Wichita, Kansas plant that has produced Wonder Waterwheels since 1945 has been received."

Before you say (or write) a word, know exactly what the writer needs from you (or what you need from the writer). Read the letter at least twice whenever the meaning is not entirely clear the first time. Then plan your answer. Will you tell your reader what he or she wants to know?

A good device is to mark in the margin of each letter the salient points which require direct comment. Another system is to go through the pile of letters numbering each one, and write brief notations keyed to the numbers. At dictation time, the notes on your pad will be valuable guidelines.

Whether a letter is to be in answer to another or for any other purpose, certain factors should run through your mind as viable questions. In time, the answers will come with a kind of automatic output. The questions are: Who? What? Where? When? Why and How?

Who Is Receiving Your Letter?

Let us begin with a look at Who is the intended recipient. Clearly you have a sensitivity to the tone of a letter received. It often reveals a personality, lifestyle, foibles and other qualities which will help you consider a proper approach, a formal or informal style. On the other hand, you may be influenced by a previous evaluation of the status or occupation of the person to whom you are writing.

Does this recognition of the Who take too much time? No. You probably do it every day on a one-to-one basis with friends, associates and customers. It may not always occur to you to be as perceptive when preparing to write a letter or memo.

It is this sense of "eye contact" (in print), that is an essential part of your own mental and emotional preparation to write.

Even the need to apologize becomes less fearsome and more gracious when first you get yourself in the frame of mind to say "I'm sorry," and know to whom and for what purpose you must write this type of letter. The result is an easy-flowing courtesy and sincerity that usually commands respect in the most uncomfortable situation.

What Must Be Written?

Knowing Who leads the way to a greater understanding of What must be written.

Informative material that carries real conviction results from the use of everything you know about your business, wherever it is feasible or applicable. Given the necessary background of facts, one should write equally well a sales letter, an advertisement, a report, or manual of business policy. Full knowledge also fosters a flexibility of choice.

First, what is the main point and what do you need to cover it? What is the gist of the communication you have received? What parts of it pertain to the central theme? What will invite continued dialogue, and is it necessary or desirable to do so?

Elemental? Of course. Yet many business persons place too much emphasis on what they *want* to write and not enough on what *needs* to be written. For best results, it is far better to *want* to write what *needs* to be written and to know What makes the difference.

A sophisticated approach takes into account the complexities of the subject matter as viewed by the reader. There are many in this word-weary world who don't know What they're writing about and others who don't know What they're reading.

Where Is the Information?

Much of this could be avoided by a simple process that involves a preliminary use of the intellect. Where is the point of information that momentarily escapes you? Find it now. In the midst of actual writing, such probing can be a nerve-wracking, time-consuming obtrusion.

Under stress, there is a temptation to drift into a kind of pretension rather than take the time to assemble the needed facts. "Faking it" can be disastrously discernible by most readers. Your in-advance planning will prevent such occasions.

When Is the Best Time To Write That Letter?

A letter should be viewed as a communication tool that does by mail (or electronic message delivery) what you would do in person if time and money permitted. Therefore, good timing is another plus factor. It is well demonstrated in most business operations. Why not in written communication?

When was the message sent to you and When will you reply? When is a specific action expected or advisable? When should your employees receive that important memo about a pay increase? Will further delay in sending out sales letters hamper the seasonal demand for a product or service? Should the letter refusing credit, or saying *no* to demands, or persuading another to take action be timed in accord with an anticipated change in company policy?

Only administrative judgment can ably determine the When of important communication. Ultimately, there are probably more letters you *should* write than letters you *must* write at any given time.

Why Are You Writing?

And then there is the foremost question to be answered long before words find their way to paper: Why? Why was the message sent to you, Why are you replying or Why is there a need to make an initial contact in writing? The reason(s) probably will determine the choice of words and information.

Few people really take the trouble to write well (or do anything else) if they have not found a reason that will satisfy their own needs. Others, in their haste, neglect to notice an important element of a letter received (especially if it's poorly written), or a factor that should have been conveyed to the reader but slipped by long before it could be useful. Somewhere the purpose was lost or mislaid—and the answer to Why withered.

How Should the Message Be Delivered?

Sometimes one cannot know what to do until there is a decision as to How to do it.

For instance, was the message sent to you by Special Delivery, or by hand? Does this imply a certain urgency for a reply? How should your response be sent? By the same method, and for the same reasons? How can your

message best be transmitted if time is a prime consideration? Would a phone call be as thorough and as accurate
as the situation requires? Should a particular commitment be in writing and, if so, how should it be worded? It
is for you to judge in the light of each situation and
before writing.

The You Approach

How is the You Approach used to establish and sustain reader interest? Let it be known by frequent
references to the reader that your top-level concern is for
his or her needs and wants. Use the pronoun *you* as often
as possible, sprinkle a minimum of *I*s and *we*s only when
necessary and the effect will satisfy the reader's worst
doubts.

The Words You Choose Are You

Your letters and memos are permanent records of
your promises and progress in relation to those within
and outside the corporate structure. They are you.

When we do not choose wisely from among the many
words used in our speech, we resort to digging for less
familiar words. Then bombast is apt to set in and exact
meanings become blurred. Be direct; be original; but insist that the natural flow of correct words be under controlled conditions.

Dr. Johnson O'Connor, director of the Human Engineering Laboratory, believes that knowledge of the exact meanings of words accompanies success.

Getting it all together also means thinking first how
to use the exact meanings of words primarily to avoid
misinterpretation. The noted author, Robert Louis
Stevenson gave us a rule to remember: *Write not so*

much to be understood, but that you cannot possibly be misunderstood.

How can we use words as tools to convey thoughts, not obscure them? How can we avoid losing the reader in a mire of big-word and wordy businessese?

Aren't you tired of *expediting, finalizing* and *utilizing*? Do you keep *pipelines open, iron out bottlenecks* and frequently use *parameter*—a mathematical term—when you mean *perimeter?*

There are also hundreds of prefabricated, wordy expressions such as *best-laid plans, agree to disagree, each and everyone, acknowledge receipt of* and *owing to the fact that.*

The worst are catchall words. If allowed to run wild, they can obscure an idea or try to hide the fact that there was no idea at all. They make it possible to construct a whole letter without saying anything. *Field, factor, aspect, type, point, circumstance,* etc., seem to be doing yeoman duty in the business world.

When you are planning to write, there is a multitude of familiar clichés and pompous phrases waiting to be called. Pretend they don't exist. You don't need old "crutches." Fresh substitutes stimulate your thinking and shorten as well as strengthen your message.

As an example, when *with reference to* sneaks around the corner of your mind, think *about*—shorter and faster. Try *since* for *inasmuch as,* and the little *for* instead of *for the purpose of.* There's more of this in Chapter 4. Identify those you use the most and you'll find it easy to kick the habit.

Say What You Mean

It may come as a shock or just a reminder: some

words don't mean what you think you mean. An example: *claim* means to demand a thing as a right. Avoid its use in the sense of assert or declare.

Wrong: They claim there is an error.

Right: They declare (or assert) there is an error.

Indicate, a word dearly beloved by business writers, does not mean *to hint* or *to intimate.* Among the other expressions in common usage for the wrong intentions are *in connection with* and *represent.* Unless there is a deliberate need to be disturbingly vague, it is better to know that the purpose of a visit from an official is not *in connection with* but rather to investigate the shortages.

In ordinary business situations, everyone knows that corporate managers have the outstanding ability to be decisive. Why then are there so many messages peppered with inflated statements that sound vague? Such a tiresome expression as "This represents a change in policy" when changed to "This *is* a change in policy" is emphatic. And that's what most corporate decision-makers intend to be!

There are also dozens of little words that automatically move right along in habitual comfort on to reams of company paper. Leading the march is the overused, abused *state.* Why not substitute *say, mention, write, inform, assert,* etc., each time *state* enters the mind?

Limp words and excess verbiage cannot possibly form sentences with the kind of crisp style that commands interest. They slow the pace and impair continuity. How do you develop good sentence construction and proper word usage to give a smooth movement to coherent thoughts?

Have a repertoire of fresh words from which to choose. Then use them discreetly to produce correctly constructed sentences that say what you mean and mean what you say. If your wordage wanders, tighten the structure; be your own editor. A certain complexity of thinking probably was the basic cause of losing continuity.

Be Concise

Conciseness is the keynote that eliminates ponderous, tiresome passages. Fortunately, knowledgeable executive secretaries, in the position to influence business writing policy, are adept at weeding out the bombast and blunders. If permitted, they will extract such bearded, barnacled phrases as "beg to advise," "as per your letter," "Thanking you again," "We beg to remain," etc.

A sense of directness evolves only from the simplicity of thoughts and words. When the message is "on target," readers feel they are being written at—and they like it.

Simple Is Strong

When one's thoughts are too bookish, bits of bombast seep into the writing. Some connectives, although grammatically correct, increase pomposity. For instance, *accordingly* and *consequently* have become harsh from overuse. Soften the tone with a simple *and so*. Others include *nevertheless* (but), *more specifically* (for example), *in addition* (besides, also) and many more you will find in Chapter 4.

It is a misconception that simplicity lessens whatever "voltage" may be required in special instances. When there is occasion for deliberate hedging or double meanings for extraordinary reasons, use the power of simple words and finely-honed sentences judiciously.

Remember, however, that all writing has an enduring quality. What slides by weakly in speech remains forever strong in writing.

Those who may be in a new position or facing a new situation, may feel inhibited when called upon to make a commitment in writing. Again, a pre-game warm-up to concentrate on the proper manipulation of words usually builds confidence in one's own ability to be firm, decisive and immediately understood.

For the more extroverted, who really like to write or dictate, and do so at a fever pitch, a brief mental probe will simply guide them through their worst (and secret) doubts. Their natural drive to a strong and steady communication effort should not be affected.

In essence, clear writing is the outgrowth of clear thinking. In the business world especially, it is direct, brief, vigorous, structured—and sensible.

True ease in writing comes from art, not chance,
As those move easiest who have learn'd to dance.
'Tis not enough no harshness gives offense.
The sound must seem an echo to the sense.
                                             Alexander Pope

When thought is too weak to be simply expressed, it's clear proof that it should be rejected.
— Marquis de Vauvenargues

3.

Moving Right Along

Anatomy of an Opener and a Close

Mr. Pincham of Pincham, Pettam, Poppum and Potter calls the firm of Perkins, Parkins, Peckham and Potts and asks to speak with Mr. Perkins.

The switchboard operator, after being assured Mr. Pincham wishes to contact Mr. Perkins and not Mr. Parkins, opens the line to the proper office and announces there is a call for Mr. Perkins. The secretary will "see if he is in" and, as is customary, ask, and be told, who is calling.

That much cleared, the conversation moves more briskly: "Just one moment. Here's Mr. Perkins, put Mr. Pincham on, please," says the secretary to the operator who returns to the caller: "O.K. with Perkins, Parkins, Peckham and Potts, Mr. Pincham. Go ahead."

"'Lo, Joe? How about lunch?"

"O.K."

Familiar? Sure, it happens every day in the best of business offices, but such a roundabout way to "get through" to the real purpose of a *written* communication is far less tolerated. A reader can easily "hang up" on the opening of a letter such as this:

"I ask for your thoughtful response in reply to the information as herein outlined should you feel so inclined, and your provocative thoughts and consideration of this matter will be communicated to those who share this concern."

At the onset, the message drowns in the excess wordage. There's little chance of it resurfacing to interest the reader in the subsequent information. What the writer wanted from the reader should have been expressed simply and cordially:

"Your response to the following information would be most interesting to everyone who shares your concern."

A good opening scores on five major points:

1) It immediately puts the reader into a clear and uncluttered picture.

2) The tone is courteous, understanding, sincere and intended to create good will.

3) It gives the reader a quick grasp of the message's intent. Without delay, the basic purpose is defined and the reader knows some action is being taken.

4) The flattery of a simple adjective (note *interesting* above) puts the reader in a receptive frame of mind for the supportive information to follow the opening sentence(s).

5) It establishes the "keynote" that will forecast the trend of the entire letter and contribute to its unity and coherence.

The Salutation

The salutation, too, plays an important role. For the most part, its form is a matter of policy or dependent on secretarial know-how and, most recently, may be influenced by the vagaries of the feminist movement.

With due respect to my zealous sisters, the transmutation of "Gentlemen" into "Gentle Persons" has not won popular acceptance. No reasonable substitute has yet been found for general use although "Friends" or "Dear Friends" is a good try, but not always suitable. Happily, few letters are addressed solely to a corporation. (For more on "The Art of De-Sexing," see Chapter 6.)

The depersonalized salutation should be avoided whenever possible. "Dear Sir," "Dear Madam," (or even "Dear Ms.") is senseless when, with a little more effort, you probably could find out the name of the person or the title of the department, i.e. "Sales Department" or someone's specific title: "Purchasing Agent." Also, "Attention: Mr. _____, Mrs. _____ or Ms. _____" usually is awkward and unnecessary.

Dear plus the appropriate name is the customary form. However, there are a few among the ultra-cautious who consider *Dear* to be too intimate a greeting, as does Jimmy Carter. He eschews its literal meaning by a formula that eliminates *Dear* from the salutations of the letters he signs. According to a White House secretary, *Dear* was not to be used during the Carter administration except in "the most personal of circumstance." "To (and the name)" has been adopted by a number of administration officials who may yet set a standard for business writing in this regard.

If you're not ready to follow suit, there are two other more popular methods. One is by no salutation at all (and thus no complimentary close). This Simplified Form simply begins with "John Jones." Correct as it may be, it does give a cold tone to a greeting.

The other is a "headline salutation." If you really want a different format, this gets the letter off to an impressive start. The opener is usually about half as long as the next topic sentence and is a part of it.

"Yes, Mr. Jones . . .

. . . your new Pontiac has been ordered. It should be in by next Friday" is informative and friendly. Another example is the headline-type that leads with "Have you forgotten Ms. Smith . . ." straight into a gentle reminder of an unpaid bill.

Whatever you do, keep the reader's name in first; don't carry it to the second line. Continue the thought of the first right through the second and onward. In this format, put the name and address at the bottom so as not to divert attention from your unique salutation. As this letter form is used more often, we will overlook its apparent contrivance in favor of results.

When you receive a letter from someone who does not indicate his or her sex and you are puzzled about how to respond, check the first line of the inside address. Use the name exactly as given; don't guess. If it is "Tracy Jones" you should write "Dear Tracy Jones," to avoid looking foolish or offending someone.

Setting the Tone

You can't go too far wrong with the right attitude.

Any type of salutation should denote a "handshake" as you move into the topic sentence that sets both intent and tone.

The tone of a business communication is directly related to and dependent upon the attitude of the writer. It may be angry, reserved, serious, friendly or cordial; it may be sarcastic or condescending. The worst attitudes should never be reflected at all especially in the opening because it will pervade the entire letter.

Instead, the opening statement that firmly reveals an attitude of personal understanding will enlist the quick interest or the willing cooperation of the reader.

Whenever possible, tell the readers what they want to know, right at the beginning. For instance, why keep eager correspondents in suspense when you plan to grant or refuse favors?

Example: "You will be glad to know our Loan Officer granted your request for a 30-day extension in which to pay the next installment of $140." Or: "I am sorry to tell you that our Loan Officer cannot grant your request . . . at this time."

Then move on to support the topic sentence with more details and explanation, if required, while maintaining the cordial tone. Through the tone of your correspondence, you can help keep cooperative friends, or convert them into negative clients who would not recommend your product or service to others.

Of course, there are situations that call upon corporate strategy. Sometimes, it seems imperative to discourage further dealings with a company or a customer. In this case, lead into it more gently; perhaps with a small bit of cordial hedging in the opening sentences.

Save your "best shot" for later where it is apt to be noticed after gaining momentum from a compelling opening.

If you play it smart, however, your relationship with every respondent will appear to be friendly, but firm, and never out of control—especially on paper!

Under ordinary circumstances, the interest to be expressed should be considered as mutual, not individual. A letter that establishes an entirely selfish point of view in the opening remains offensive, whereas an opening written in a cooperative sense enlists support and attention. The key to making a good opening statement is in *knowing what fact would be of most interest to the reader.*

Many business writers enjoy telling only their own version of a story. *Communication* means more than telling someone something. It's derived from the Latin root word *communicare* meaning "to share," as in *communion.* It's a two-way process: what we say (or write) and what the other person understands. You begin that interplay before and within the opening, as you put yourself in the place of the one with whom you communicate.

Most everyone knows that the rush and pressures of executive obligations tend to spawn hints of "Isn't-it-great-this-guy/gal-gets-a-letter-at-all." As a result, thousands of men and women every day receive too-casual replies from executives who probably feel that any answer is better than none.

Assume that someone submits a proposal to your department. An answer is expected, whenever its fate is decided.

So you write something like this: "In reviewing your

proposal and pertinent remarks, we are carefully deliberating the economic feasibility of the endeavor."

This, of course, is usually followed by equally non-committal businessese that fails to provide any answer to the when, how and why questions provoked by the ambiguous opening. Of course, you didn't have any answers at the time, but you did give the person the courtesy of an immediate reply—however obtuse it may have been.

Would it have been better to wait for a little more information? Then write: "Thank you for submitting a most interesting proposal. The cost factors, in particular, are being determined by our Executive Committee and a decision should be reached within the week." In this way, you do not dangle by saying nothing, but you do give hope that will comfortably sustain the reader until the final decision is reached.

Some Necessary Openings

There are other situations, certainly less tense, when some deviation from the normal pattern of an opening must be excused in the interest of operational efficiency.

For filing purposes or the tracing of files, a full sentence may be needed to identify the letter properly with the general subject. If you must refer to dates, file numbers, amounts, etc., try to bury it inside the sentence. Otherwise, the letter carries a cold tone and you are tempted to open with a hackneyed, "Acknowledging receipt of your letter of June 10. . . ."

Use the You Approach, "Thank you for your letter of June 10" or "You certainly will receive our full cooperation when the procedure as outlined by material in File #482, dated June 10, 1979, is approved."

Then set the trend in the *next* sentence as you would normally do in the first sentence of an opening. Discuss the subject without the clutter of required material. This secondary topic sentence somewhat relieves the bluntness of the first that might have "turned off" the reader.

The topic sentence acts as a guide in keeping the discussion within bounds. If the central thought is buried too deeply within the letter, coherence is likely to be poor. Your opening sets the pace for progressive stages from beginning to end. This is why the most difficult part of the message may be the starting point because you know it must occupy an emphatic position. Its clearness and conciseness often determines the reader's understanding of the entire effort.

The You Approach—Again

A letter that opens with a stereotyped expression begins its life in a weak and decidedly unemphatic condition. "In reply to your letter . . . ," "In reference to your esteemed favor . . . ," "In pursuance to our telephone conversation . . . ," are only a few of the ancient phrases slowly, but surely dying in the business world.

Openings such as: "It was interesting to learn from your letter (call) . . . ," or "Thank you for letting me know . . . ," are the natural outgrowth of our consideration for the reader. And that's what its all about—the You Approach either directly or implied.

The You Approach works best when it cannot be construed by the reader as a manufactured form of flattery. The quality of its use stems from the ability of the writer to identify sincerely with the reader. A *your* forcibly inserted into "your proposal," "your letter," etc., offers only a dab of brightness because it will appear to be contrived.

Giving the reader the full spotlight by a too liberal use of "you" and "yours" is a habit of those who regard this device as a cover-up for the lack of other important writing techniques. Most importantly, this over-use of a good thing annoys most astute readers.

In moderation, the You Approach can be a valuable tool for a variety of purposes especially those which call for persuasion or the handling of situations requiring extraordinary diplomacy.

For instance, many business engagements are made by telephone, but often confirmed by letter. "As you requested, the time and date for the presentation of your marketing program has been set for July 1 at 10 A.M." This adds more personal value to the confirmation than "The marketing program I discussed during our telephone conversation can be presented promptly at 10 A.M. on July 1."

The You Approach is especially effective when dealing with an angry customer or associate. Even the first words can begin to develop good will where none may have existed or where it had been slightly damaged.

Putting yourself right into the reader's place, you might answer: "This is the answer to your problem..." or "It's easy to understand how you feel; many people feel the same way when...." Here you identify with another's problem; show that you "give-a-damn" simply by using words gently.

We or I?

Choosing the proper pronoun can help create the proper impression. Will it be *we* or *you*? Either one of these pronouns can be carried to extremes—*we* to the extent of selfishness, *you* to artificiality.

Once the writing begins with a *we*, there's a good chance the entire letter will suffer from "we-itis": a succession of sentences such as "We know you will find...," "We have been aware of the need...," "We want you to remember...."

As Mark Twain said: "Only presidents, editors and people with tapeworms have the right to use the editorial 'we.'"

When you really mean *I*, and would rather write *we*, the easy way might be (and too often is): "The *writer....*" In either a personal or corporate sense, this is a substitute as objectionable as the fault itself.

Thus, use *we*, not editorially, but when it is obvious that only the company, a group, a department, etc., can perform the action. "Yes, we can supply 5,000 brochures..." is correct usage.

The Challenge To Be "Different"

The opening of a letter can also be a challenge to your creativity. You may be the executive who has a desire to be a professional writer. Your letters and memos are probably "different"; real head-on, splashy, experimental in style and format and each designed to attract maximum attention.

This labored attempt to be "different," especially during the opening thrust, seems to satisfy only the writer's creative urge.

A top executive should be different because he or she has learned to write to *express*, not to *impress* with clever verbiage that rivals the talents of advertising copywriters. The basic rules of the business-writing game are far simpler to follow.

The time to be "different" in the best sense, is when it is least expected. When you're itching to "wield the ax" at an ill employee whose work projects are behind schedule, or the vendor who misplaced your order when his wife ran off with the neighbor, be "different"; be sympathetic.

Don't chastise them with the first blow; work up to it gradually—and graciously. Beginning with "Your recent problem is unfortunate . . . but . . ." will go a long way toward constructive action or desired results.

Try the Apologetic Opening

Also, when warranted, an apologetic opening is not only a great attention-getter (since it's rarely expected), but leads the way logically and easily into a plausible explanation of a situation or a method of resolving a problem that is mutually ageeable.

SMOOTH: "I am sorry, Mr. Smith, that the credit investigation seemed indiscreet to you. The manager sincerely hopes you will accept this explanation for making inquiries."

ROUGH: "Your recent complaint about our credit check is unjustified. You should regard this as company procedure. Discontinuance of the practice would result in accepting orders from all those who are not capable of meeting their financial obligations."

The first opening began with an empathetic approach that warms-up the reader for a follow-up that explains why your company's action was not intended to offend anyone. The abrupt, uncompromising tone of the second version is obvious. It could only further alienate the customer.

How difficult it is to place ourselves on common ground with claimants, complainers and those to whom we must deny a favor! As you know, each one expects you to have a deep personal understanding and some psychic knowledge of his or her preferred treatment.

This is why not all beginnings can be purely empathetic. Nor can they defer the main point. Sometimes, a reversal of the usual order is more appropriate.

Some hard-nosed business persons want to "know the worst" right at the start. Therefore, an obliging practice is to state the denial, regretfully of course, at the outset.

The explanation to follow may seem anti-climatic and weakened by the contrast but you may prefer that it not be read too attentively anyhow. Your fine business judgment will determine the method of devising an approach in accord with your knowledge or perception of the reader's preference.

Humor Isn't Always Funny

Being "different" also takes the form of humor. Unless your comedic sense is extraordinary, a funny opening can "bomb." If you know the reader has great respect for your wit, the risk lessens. Otherwise, seeming foolish, especially in writing, is rarely worth the effort.

Nevertheless, there may be times when you cannot resist the clever joke or simile to get the letter started or brighten your day. Just remember you're writing a letter not making a speech.

Be sure of the objective; incorporate the funny, if you must, into a topic sentence. Make it relevant to the main point, but proceed with caution. This, too, takes discretion.

Compliments Are Welcome

There is a magic word, however, that is always relevant to the subject and purpose of a letter or memo. It soars to the psyche of all people whenever appropriate and makes a rewarding beginning. The word is *Congratulations!*

If a business associate, customer or community leader is worthy of kudos, your direct and prompt mention of the accomplishment will make an everlasting impression.

It's all part of a business decorum we know so well. Openings that flatter or compliment are prime attention-getters and most always motivate readers to become more interested in whatever you write (and do).

Nevertheless, flattery must be judicious and sensible. Generally, there is greater risk in flattering important persons who, having heard it all before, are turned off by comments they assume are phony.

Compliments are more enduring.

At a dinner given in his honor, Chauncey Depew was the recipient of many compliments from various speakers. Replying, the famed legislator began, "It's pleasant to hear these nice words while I'm still alive. I'd rather have the taffy than the epitaphy."

The Art of Persuasion

Although the art of persuasion is familiar to executives who manage subordinates and other associates on a one-to-one basis, persuasion-in-writing seems more difficult.

The design of a good opening can be blocked psychologically by the awesome responsibility of persuading another human being to do something that may not be appealing. Don't let it happen; anticipate a result that is inevitable when all goes well because you have found the right words to convince the reader.

Simply avoid the old temptation to think, "*I can persuade.*" The more satisfying pattern is *how he or she can be persuaded.* This will help you pitch the opening in particular to the other person's emotions—*not your own.* The rest should follow in good order.

As in any communication, take a hard look at the first sentence or paragraph and ask yourself: "Is it getting through?" "Have I begun to interest this person in the benefits. . . ."

To illustrate: "Your extended knowledge of our various insurance plans could easily lead to an association with the XYZ Company that could fully meet your needs." This makes a sales opening on the first show and also a good personal and corporate impression.

Letters are judged by the same standards as any personal introduction to another person. Would you ridicule or belittle or question judgment, honesty or sincerity in your greeting of a new (or old) friend?

This happens sometimes in letters which have a beginning, middle and end all rolled into one opening statement or two. Example: "You told us you had paid the last installment on your loan. We have learned that you did not."

Is it not better to give the reader—either friend or foe—the benefit of the doubt? "Not many people like to remember loan payments. And I'm sure that is why you forgot to send yours along." And continue: "We quite understand and will be able to update our records when you send us your check."

Collection letters, of course, are among the most difficult, not only to write completely, but to approach with the attitude that satisfies. As in any communication, if you cannot relate to the reader right at the beginning, start over.

A Happy Ending

If you cannot relate to the reader right at the beginning, switch the attitude, hold the thought, and start over. A good beginning is likely to lead to a better ending. And when the time comes to end the visit, don't bolt out the door or stand in the doorway after you've said goodbye. Leave gracefully.

A needlessly prolonged ending, weak ending, ungracious ending, or an ending that has no meaning at all can put a damper on the overall effect.

To bring a communication to a smooth stop choose one of two broad categories of endings: those which ask for action and those designed to impress the reader but don't require action.

A simple device that serves either purpose is to pluck the main idea from the body of the piece and reinforce it—concisely, emphatically and, whenever possible, in different words. If the project is lengthy, conclude with a summary of the main points. As any good teacher knows, "Tell them once, tell them again, and then tell them what you told them," but only by condensing and rephrasing.

Especially when the subject requires some negative

tone always be positive in your closing. Any ending should serve as a punch line, even if it isn't a joke!

For sales-oriented letters, the ending that carries a value judgment can tie up the pitch nicely. Example: "Our company, as the leader in the highly competitive oil industry, is in an enviable position to offer broader opportunities for sound investments."

Or, stress succinctly the potential effect of your ideas: "Those who invest in our company will share in our profits." A simple statement of fact: "You are always welcome whenever you stop by" puts a warm kind of sell in your ending.

When you ask for ACTION do not use warmed-over clichés such as "Trusting you will give this matter your prompt attention," "Hoping to hear from you soon," "Please call us if we can be of further service." (This one frequently is tossed in when no service whatever was offered.)

"May I hear from you soon?" or "If you'd like more information, won't you let me know?" are somewhat stereotyped, but suitable only because they ask a question. Questions do provoke reaction and carry a potential for action.

If you need specific action, the ending must tell the reader What, When and How without being offensively redundant. Again, use the question form: "Would you place your order by April 6 to beat the seasonal rush and take advantage of our special rate?"

The conclusion that carries a personal note of good will strengthens the You Approach. For instance: "It is a pleasure to add your name to our list of customers, Mr. Smith," or "Best wishes for a most successful meeting at the Chicago conference."

When writing to a friend, there's no rule against adding a personal comment to the letter's business message. Loosen up, ask about members of the reader's family, a mutual friend, health, future plans, or use the space to make a luncheon date. It may be worth the extra effort.

Whatever words are used to make an ending, leave the reader with a favorable impression that will be remembered. Words ring loudest during the last part of the message. Don't add anything to dim the sound.

Endings such as "Thanking you in advance" or "Trust that this will meet with your approval" are like radar bouncing back from an iceberg.

Generally, closings with irrelevant statements such as "Yours very truly" carry no punch. It's an outmoded inanity that has no political, historical nor personal significance in most cases.

Strangely, a leading secretarial handbook advocates the use of "Yours very truly" when there is NO personal connection and "sincerely" only for personal letters. Regardless of handbook advice, "sincerely" now is the popular closing for any letter that reflects sincerity by its simplicity of language and tone. Most do.

"Sincerely" really means there is no intended "cover-up"; your communication is "sine cera" (without wax). Roman craftsmen commonly used the term when they obscured the chips in ancient statues with wax. It covers the subject nicely.

When you want to be more specific, choose any closing that reinforces the thrust and tone of your letter, conveys a realistic thought and does not break the attention you have built. No closing should be so exuberant as to lift readers off their chairs, but a little imagination will help to keep them there.

Any communication will bring results when you and the reader remain together from the beginning through the ending and both of you are satisfied. Why risk the potential benefits of that satisfaction?

Gobbledygook: wordy and generally unintelligible jargon. Webster's New Collegiate Dictionary. *Maury Maverick, former Congressman from Texas is credited with coining the word to make it sound like turkey-talk.*

4.

Solecism and Other Sins

How Words Work For or Against You

In just three words, "Veni, vidi, vici" or "I came, I saw, I conquered," Julius Caesar described his triumph in 47 B.C. over Pharnaces II, King of Pontus.

Here's a 20th-century translation in exaggerated business jargon:

"I made my propitious appearance on the site in question and in this respect conceptualized the conditions as related to the parameter of the impending situation and, subsequently, proceeded to affect an implementation of the projected process that ultimately resulted in the crushing finalization of the confrontation without further delay and in my favor."

Wake Up Your Words and Weigh Them

Surely you talk simply, interestingly and, most always, correctly, but in the throes of writing administrative material, you may become like archaic executives who would *say* they get ready to leave, but *write* that they are preparing to depart.

It's all so simple to spray words on paper: "Jack Brown has offered a suggestion regarding a departure from our standard procedure with respect to renumeration of overtime employment."

Why not, "Jack Brown suggests a new way to pay for overtime."?

Further, there are many other uniforms of speech in the business world that are becoming tiresome. It seems any change in personnel becomes a "shakeup"; standard procedure for making a suggestion is to "drop a hint"; defeats are "crushing"; changes in the existing system are "noble experiments" or "dangerous departures"; most every risk is "calculated" and one is not "suspended," but "takes administrative leave."

The public has also grown tired of bastard words that screech like chalk across a blackboard. There are *eggheads, do-gooders,* and *high-type* men and women who *think modern* and *set targets budgetwise* to *customize, permatize, winterize or bulletinize.* And could we "complete" or "conclude" instead of *finalize* once in a while?

Other executive favorites, such as *archetype, concept, elitist, ambiance* and *polarization,* are legitimate when properly used, but usually inspire heavy supportive rhetoric.

Authoritative wordsmiths say words should average

about 150 syllables for each 100 words (or one or two syllable words) for maximum readability.

The super-psuedo intellectual, however, also likes to use short, but fancy words such as *indite* when simply *compose, write, direct* or *dictate* is meant and *resile* rather than *withdraw* from a purpose.

The same person may *confabulate* with familiar talk; call a fraudulent abstraction of money (embezzlement) a *defalcation,* and most always *plans in advance* (*advance* is superfluous).

Reader's Digest advises its writers to limit sentences to 20 words. Other reading specialists say sentences of 17 words or less are the most easily understood.

In business writing, especially, extra words are thrown in for no good reason. For instance, these words (shown in parenthesis) are redundant and thus, have no real value:

> as a (usual) rule
> at 9 a.m. (in the morning)
> cooperate (together)
> (important) essentials
> (joint) partnership
> total effect (of all this)
> close to (the point of) bankruptcy
> circulated (around)
> different (in various ways)
> if and when (drop either the *if* or *when*).

Long sentences may bore and confuse readers, but a flagrant misuse of words is a major attack on clarity. Exact meanings of words are most important.

Even Mrs. Noah Webster misused a word. One day

she saw her husband kissing their maid. "Noah," she exclaimed, "I'm surprised."

"Oh no, my dear," replied the author of the famous dictionary. "I am *surprised.* You are *astonished.*" (Astonished means amazed; surprised, in one sense, means caught in the act.)

There are many words that have become so overused in the business world, one tends to forget their real meanings. Here are a few of the most popular:

Firm should not refer to a corporation or company. A firm is a partnership which has no standing in law as an entity distinct from its members in the way a corporation is a legal person.

Concern is a business or manufacturing organization, not a professional one. (Now use *firm*) "He is a member of a legal concern in New York" is incorrect.

About is redundant if a figure is explicitly stated to be an estimate or is implicitly presented as an approximation in the form of a round number. "This month's production was estimated at ~~about~~ 640,000."

Mitigate really means *moderate* or *soften.* It is incorrectly used when the writer has *militate* in mind, which means "have effect, for or against." Thus, "An official ruling *mitigates* against eventual cancellation of overtime compensation," is incorrect.

Element, factor, feature, phase have four distinct meanings and are not interchangeable. *Element* means a component part. (Honesty is an *element* of the banker's character.) *Factor* means one of a number of elements or conditions that make up a whole thing. (An important *factor* in determining the shipping date is the supply of materials.) *Feature* means a very evident characteristic. (The outstanding *feature* of this plan is its flexibility.) *Phase* means one aspect of a situation or set of conditions. (The second *phase* of the process leads us to believe it can be cost-controlled.)

Virtually is often used in place of *actually*. It means in essence or in effect; *actually* means in fact, really. Correct: "When your lawyer speaks for you, you are *virtually* speaking yourself, even though you are not *actually* present."

Try editing copies of your most recent letters. Not only will you recognize other words for which there are better substitutes, but you will become more sensitive to the word-weeds that cramp your natural style. Run your pen through words and phrases that serve no real purpose. Whatever remains probably is all you need to write.

Let's try it with these typical sentences:

Please ~~feel free to~~ write ~~to us~~ if you ~~find yourself in~~ need ~~of~~ more information.

If ~~at any time whatsoever~~ we can be of further service ~~to you, kindly do not hesitate to please~~ let us know.

~~Per your request, you will find~~ (E) enclosed (is) the information you requested (.) ~~on our services.~~

~~This will acknowledge with thanks~~ (Y) your letter ~~of March 1, 1979 commending our effort in your behalf and~~ it is ~~very~~ much appreciated.

~~Complying with your request of recent date, you will find~~ (A) attached (is) a copy of our ~~very~~ latest price list (.) ~~for your perusal.~~

May we ~~ask that you kindly permit us to~~ place your name on our mailing list?

Synonyms for Strength

You may also be shocked to learn that you unwittingly appear to be one who wishes or begs when neither was your intent.

Do you write: I *wish:* to state, to call your attention, to notify, to thank or I *beg:* to inform you, to advise you or ask you to consider this matter?

Wishing and begging never won (or lost) a game. Readers, like sports fans, look for action. So ingrained is the habit of using these weak words, we tend to forget their true meanings.

Also, *hope* and *trust* roll onto paper before we catch them. In most cases, *believe, surely* or *am certain* are admirable substitutes that add variety and verve and—say what you mean.

Synonym-searching is most obvious somewhere around the middle of a writing exercise. That's where the issues become cloudy and a bit of boredom sets in. The message then babbles by a repetition of the same words. More often, it is burdened by stilted, over-used words for which there are simple synonyms.

Here are a few overused words that should be retired in favor of more informal expressions (in parenthesis):

advise (say, tell)
ascertain (find out)
concerning (about)
desire (want)
eliminate (omit)
forthwith (now, at once, promptly)
inasmuch (since, as)
initial (first)
necessitate (need, force)
patronage (business)
pursuant (according to)
retain (keep)
expedite (hasten)
furnish (give)
henceforth (after this)
secure (get)
ultimate (final)

Writing Can Be Overeducated

The too-literate can twist and turn large sentences like rubber bands in order to express what may be a tiny idea. The worst writing is done by the best educated, according to most critics of writing in the United States.

This comes as a shock to recent graduates who soon discover there is little use for their splendid literary rhetoric in the real world. Sadly, the B.A., M.B.A., or Ph.D. that may move them into management positions does not necessarily reflect their ability to write a letter or report in the "business way."

This is evidenced by the reports of corporate trainers who are busier than ever. William H. Kitchelt Jr., Departmental Trainer, E.I DuPont de Nemours Co., says the neophytes must be told: "When the tablecloth is red, there's no other way to say it."

Grammar and Usage

This sensible approach clarifies all the guidelines for effective writing. There are certain standards that command the respect of those who are in a position to pass authoritative judgment. These include many of your customers and associates, as well as recognized grammarians.

Good usage in English is based on a mastery of the meaning, pronunciation and spelling of words and phrases. Webster defines usage as "the way in which a word, phrase, etc., is used to express a particular idea." Unlike grammar, good usage is not absolutely standardized; it does permit a preference, provided that preference is grammatically correct.

Grammar, a system of rules which deals with the forms of words and their arrangement in sentences, is separate from usage. Nevertheless, certain details of grammar, such as the parts of speech, are referred to quite often in discussions of usage. In concert, both are essential to effective writing.

Active or Passive

Let us begin by considering verbs as they are used actively or passively. A verb is said to be in the *active* voice when a person or thing *performs* an action; it is said to be in the *passive* voice when the person or thing *receives* the action, or is acted upon.

Sentences lose their power when we lapse into the passive voice. On the corporate level, the habit flourishes thoughtlessly.

As examples: nobody ever *does* anything; things happen. One does not refer to somebody; reference is made to. Prices rise; nobody raises them.

This may be a device to evade or shift responsibility. If that is your intent, fine; if not, convert passivity to activity. Limp words and phrases often cause disunified, unemphatic and, sometimes, offensive communication. The active voice usually makes the message clearer and more forceful.

WEAK: An important decision will be made by the president.

STRONG: The president will make an important decision.

WEAK: Good letters are written by my employer.

STRONG: My employer writes good letters.

Most changes from passive to active voice also result in the elimination of excess wordage.

"I have revised the letter," is more emphatic and obviously shorter than "A revision of the letter has been affected."

The flexibility of our language provides several other opportunities to strengthen expression. For instance, we can choose action verbs to replace those which take the muscle out of the message. As an example: "You stated that . . . " can be brightened and strengthened by choosing a simple word: "say, mention, write, inform, suggest or assert."

Adjectives also play strong roles on the active/passive scene. Using an adjective is normally more forceful than using an abstract noun to name a quality or condition. Thus, write, "He is a proud man," instead of "He is a man of pride."

Mark Twain belittled the use of the adjective when he advised: "When in doubt, leave it out." Most overuse of any of the parts of speech is more easily cured than pardoned.

That or Which

Many executives are habitual users of "that." If they would check stringy sentences more carefully, they would soon learn it is less time-consuming to eliminate unnecessary *thats* than it is to position them properly.

Also, the proper use of *that* and *which* absorbs much of their creative decisionmaking. More often, the choice is a rough guess.

For the record: the rule is: *that* is used to introduce a limiting or defining clause; *which* is used to introduce a nondefining or parenthetical clause.

If the clause could be omitted without altering the point of the sentence or if the clause could be enclosed in parentheses, it should be introduced by *which*. Otherwise use *that*.

"The Delaware River *which* flows past Wilmington, is muddy," but "The muddy river *that* flows past Wilmington is the Delaware."

Also, *which* refers to things, not persons. "The house *which* was built. . . ."

Strangely, some people think *which* is more elegant and use it where *that* should be. At times, neither word is necessary. "The contract *that* I signed two years ago states . . ." invariably will first be altered to "The contract *which* I signed. . . ." Although correct, "The contract I signed two years ago . . ." is acceptable.

In such instances, the use of *that* is optional and built on idiom. If it doesn't do something for the sentence, leave it out.

There are notable exceptions to the deletion of *that* as illustrated in this sentence: "The CIA disclosed today (that) a document that apparently contained information on a secret mission has been discovered in the hands of an unauthorized person." Inclusion of *that* as shown in parenthesis is definitely needed. Its omission changes meaning.

Nouns

Then there is the most troublesome part of speech: the noun. In a sense, it causes the biggest problems because it names a person, place or thing.

Many business writers suffer from "nominalization." It is described as an *addiction* to the overuse of nouns that robs other parts of speech of their vitality.

This should not become uncontrollable if we remember to write person to person. If we do not, nominalization provides a pompous statement like this: "It is of great importance that action be taken in respect to this matter at the earliest possible date."

The following simple conversion says what you mean with far less effort (and nouns): "It is most important that something be done about this matter as soon as possible."

Nominalization is a frequent practice of memo writers: "The purpose of this memorandum is to remind you. . . ." "This is to remind you . . ." is more effective, if necessary at all; it is a memo!

Of course, there is something this type of writer likes better than a noun: two nouns. Unions no longer vote in favor of striking; they vote in favor of "strike action." Airplanes are not grounded by bad weather; they succumb to bad "weather conditions." The words "action" and "condition" are superfluous.

Picking Phrases

Simple logic, too, will help you eliminate phrases and decide on substitutes.

For instance: why write "I acknowledge receipt of your. . . ."? If you're answering a letter, you must have received it. "Contents noted" and "above mentioned" are similarly superfluous. Also, why pad a letter with "for your information?" Is it for anyone else's information?

Other word-weeds include:

"As a matter of fact"—five unneeded words
"Please be advised that"—superfluous irony
"Take this opportunity"—scrap this, unless
   you mean it.
"Allow me to"—too solicitous, unnecessary

And those precious openers:

"Referring to the matter of . . . ," "Your favor of . . . ," "Your communication of . . . ," "Relative to . . . ," are as outmoded as "Thanking you for your continued business," too-often used as a standard closing cliché.

By using the parts of speech properly, we can be rid of other antiquated forms. Simple substitutes add emphasis, a friendly tone and cut down the extra wordage.

Here are some important "instead ofs"; the preferred word or phrase is in parentheses:

in the event that (if)
as regards (about)
permit me to thank you (thanks)
attached find (attached is)
in lieu of (in place of)
check to cover (check for)
endeavor to ascertain (to find out)
accordingly, consequently (so)
at the present writing, at this time (now)
due to the fact that (since or because)

Sentences are also strengthened and time saved when you "forget" instead of "do not remember", "distrust" instead of "do not have confidence in" and "ignore" rather than "do not pay any attention to."

Feed this compact thought, "As our policy requires..." into a dictaphone and out comes "In accordance with the requirement of our policy...."

Also, there's no difference in meaning between "to refer" and "to make reference to"; "to consider" and "to have under consideration"; "to correct" and "to take corrective action"; or "to receive" and "to be in receipt of."

Conjunctive-itis

Another debilitating exercise is to discuss all aspects of a situation in one sentence. To do this, we need conjunctions. *And* and *but* are the most popular. Such sentences should be converted to two or more, whenever possible.

STRINGY: A site has been selected in Dayton,

Ohio, for the erection of a new processing plant, but prior to preparation of the lease we are calling upon our Engineering Department to provide the usual number of prints to accompany the lease and when we receive them we will submit the lease for execution on the part of both parties."

CONCISE AND CORRECT: "A site has been selected in Dayton, Ohio, for the new processing plant.

The lease will be ready for signatures upon completion of the required prints now being prepared by our Engineering Department."

Further, too many conjunctions clutter business messages much in the same way as in spoken expressions. Do you write and say: "The project is *both* feasible and costly"? (There's no point in using *both*.) "The meeting began early *and so* we completed the agenda." (*and so* is unnecessary; choose *and* or *so*.)

Conjunctions can also make a sentence contraction more emphatic. Example: "She is not only well-educated, *but* also efficient." is a stronger characterization than "She is well-educated and efficient."

Prepositions

A preposition is less unruly than a conjunction. It connects its object (ordinarily a noun or pronoun) with another word and shows a relation between them. It does have certain distinctions in use, idiomatic tendencies and a notorious reputation for causing controversy.

If you end sentences with prepositions, join the crowd of great writers. Even language purists have stopped shuddering at Shakespeare's "We are such stuff as dreams are made *on*" and Kipling's "Too horrible to be trifled *with.*"

Sir Winston Churchill, the 1953 Nobel Prize winner for literature, replied to criticism of his "That is something I shall not put up with" by observing, "That is something up with which I shall not put."

A good test is to move the preposition from the end to another part of the sentence. If it seems too awkward or clouds the meaning, move it back.

"He's one person I simply won't do business with" is less stuffy than "He's one person with whom I simply won't do business."

"Everything depends on what the plans are meant for" usually is a more natural expression than "Everything depends on for what the plans are meant." (Advice: forget the whole thing and rewrite it to read: "Everything depends on the purpose of the plans.") A preposition is not always a bad word to end a sentence with.

To Split or Not To Split

Neither is splitting an infinitive now considered a great grammatical sin. Split it, if you must, provided it makes the sentence more accurate and less awkward.

Here is an example of when *not* to: "We must remember to thoroughly check each balance sheet." This may have been done for emphasis, but "thoroughly" could come just as satisfactorily at the end. So why split?

The modified rule says an adverb should not be placed between two parts of the infinitive unless placing the adverb elsewhere results in awkwardness. This split is awkward: "We urge you to promptly write us if we can be of help." Better: "We urge you to write us promptly if we can be of help."

Contractions

We do not always do what is permissible. For instance, there is nothing ungrammatical about contractions, yet you may carefully avoid their use in business writing.

The use of contractions is the most easily acquired and effective technique known to modern *informal* writing. Nevertheless, contractions should not be used at every opportunity. You would not write *should've* and *it'd* because they are awkward and might startle the reader.

Haven't, there's, don't and *it's* are more acceptable because they are commonly used in speech. We can safely follow the guidelines for press writers as set by *The Associated Press Style Book:* "Avoid excessive use of contractions. Contractions listed in the dictionary are acceptable, however, in informal contexts or circumstances where they reflect the way a phrase commonly appears in speech or writing."

Many publications today use contractions, especially for negative words. With the possibility that a *not* be dropped by a typesetter, a contraction would make it less likely for a meaning to be changed.

Example: (*Wall Street Journal,* Dec. 17, 1979) "The issue *hasn't* been resolved and a recall *isn't* planned in the U.S."

Many a business message, too, has gone awry

because of a *not* that was lost in transcription or overlooked by a typist. "We have (not) agreed to participate . . ." could be a disaster.

In telegrams, be more sensible the Navy way: NOT REPEAT NOT.

Contractions should be used to produce an informal writing style that speaks casually to the reader. Don't let them creep into a letter requiring a stiffer or more formal approach.

How Colloquial Can You Be?

Today's "formal informality" conveys a message smoothly from one person to another. That is why *some* colloquialisms are acceptable when they are needed to lighten the tone of certain business letters.

More often, colloquialisms, or slang, adversely affect sentence construction and violate major grammatical rules.

True, we have learned that English grammar is far more fluid and less realistic than some textbooks and many strict grammarians admit. The essential element is to know these qualities and use them to keep the rhythm of a more relaxed presentation.

Be informal but judicious and you will produce clear, concise and correct written material that gets through to readers without their loss of respect for your control of the English language.

At times it can be risky, especially when we try to mate the old and new. They are generally incompatible.

Here's an example: "We're in receipt of your letter of

June 10 and sure do beg to report I'm anticipating being in the position of shipping another order soon to wind up our contract."

Too much concentration on the formal versus the informal style tends to dim our vision of other important requirements.

Good grammar gives us the guidelines to the most coveted rewards in business writing: emphasis and clarity.

Building Sentences

Sentence construction leads the way. First, the principle of subordination must be in the mind of the writer. Balance the values of your thoughts. Then emphasize the major idea in independent clauses and the minor thought in a subordinate clause.

You may decide that a construction to lend suspense will affect a stronger climax. Example: "Though she had not applied for the position, she was promoted to supervisor," makes a valid point. "She was promoted to supervisor, though she had not applied for the position," tends to reflect your effort to just "tack on" an idea.

Placing important words and ideas first also contributes to emphasis and clarity. "I received an order for 5,000 Widgets from the XYZ Co. when I showed the 243 line on Tuesday" leaves no doubt that the order itself is of prime interest.

Parenthetical clauses and phrases belong in the middle, not at the beginning or the end.

Emphasis by repetition is rarely effective in ordinary business messages; although it is characteristic of sales letters, if employed sparingly. The "rule of three" is the most effective. The idea of a product or service mentioned more often than three times bores the reader as easily as a slogan repeated too often during a brief radio or television commercial.

Other arrangements of material also give prominence to specific passages. Price quotes and listings of items should be set apart in a letter or report whenever possible.

A short paragraph next to a paragraph of normal length, or between two such paragraphs, takes on emphasis.

Underlining, if used sparingly, is a visual device to assure emphasis.

Capitalization is effective, but should be used only for adding advertising value to a trade name. "The WONDER WIDGET is the best on the market," would be more comfortable in a sales letter.

Conversely, the use of capitals to "shout" a word or phrase in an ordinary letter text is of doubtful propriety (as is the rest of this sentence): "We are sorry, but unless your loan is placed in good standing AT ONCE, we cannot continue to carry it."

Punctuation: The Traffic Signals of Writing

Punctuation is a different matter; its power can make or break clarity.

During the 15th century, it was decided that reading material without "stop" and "go" signals was bothersome. And so symbols for sounds that represent the modulations of the voice were devised. Basically, a comma indicates a slight pause, a semicolon indicates a somewhat longer pause; and a period, a full stop. Apostrophes, exclamation points, quotation marks, etc., are self-explanatory.

The comma is the most frequently used and misused punctuation mark and the one most apt to cause run-on sentences. "With these business forecasts on your desk at the start of every week you can be prepared for the changes that are on the way," is even more tiresome with commas.

Parenthetical prepositional phrases should also be set off by commas. They begin with *with, without, in addition to,* etc.

"The sturdy construction of the machine, with a complete absence of delicate parts, makes for low operating costs," is correctly punctuated. Remove the comma after "machine" and you have a machine with a complete absence of delicate parts.

We must also be sure to set off those successive phrases that have been crowded away from the words they modify. Imagine this sentence if it did not have commas: "On the basis of today's closing prices, we can offer No. 3 Wonder Widgets at $115 a gross, in bulk, for delivery at Wilmington, Delaware, to be routed via United Parcel at Philadelphia, Pa."

Do not set off an essential participial phrase. Thus, this sentence would contain no commas: "Our company known as the Wonder Widget Works is valued at $5 million."

The absolute phrase is set off by commas: "The papers having been properly signed, we were ready to close the sale."

Use commas to separate items in a series of more than three (red, yellow, blue and green) and to indicate omissions: "He arrived April 10, (the comma here replaces the meaning 'in the year of') 1979."

When we fail to use a comma to indicate the joining of parts of a sentence, the sentence may have to be read twice. "As you know most people come again" is confusing. A comma after "know," will give you a pause.

A comma is an excellent interrupter and needed to clarify meaning. "The employees, we knew, were interested" could not be construed as "The employees we knew were interested."

A classic story best illustrates the power of the comma: Once when King Frederick the Great was offended by the philosopher Voltaire, he issued a public message: "Frederick the Great declares Voltaire is an ass."

But Voltaire "outpunctuated" the king by the insertion of two commas: "Frederick the Great, declares Voltaire, is an ass."

Semicolons are essential to avoid getting ourselves and the readers snarled up in a traffic of sentences while we continue a thought. Let us review briefly the principal uses for the semicolon:

1. *To separate a series of long clauses:* "If I am absent from work one day, I notice the difference; if I am absent for two days, my critics notice; if I am absent for three days, the entire company notices it."

2. *In a compound sentence to separate clauses not joined by a conjunction:* "Writing is easy; writing effectively is more difficult."

3. *Before a conjunctive adverb:* "It was a difficult assignment; still, it was not impossible."

In the struggle for clarity, punctuation, as all grammatical devices, is a friend, not foe.

The strongest enemies are words themselves. The worst of these are right words in the wrong places, wrong words in the right places, and words with misinterpreted meanings.

Too little respect, or none at all, for the academics of the English language has created a horde of confused writers who think they are communicating clearly and concisely.

There is no material with which we shall ever work that has as much potential energy as words.

Learn to use little words in a big way.
— Arthur Kudner

5.

From Idea to Expression

With Clarity, Unity and Coherence

Winston Churchill was noted for his precise use of the language to stress dominant ideas. Yet his famous tribute to the Royal Air Force is commonly *misquoted* as follows, "Never . . . have so many owed so much to so few."

In his actual words, Churchill put the verb in the passive voice and thus made grammar more precisely show the emphasis he wanted: "Never . . . was so much owed by so many to so few." The misquotation puts the least important idea in the important subject position.

It was Churchill's wish to express three ideas:

1) the greatness of the service performed by the RAF; 2) the small number of men who performed it; and 3) the large numbers who benefited by it.

If you keep in mind that the topic theme of the sentence is the wonderful work of the RAF, you will agree that the greatness of the service and the few men who provided it are more important than the number who benefited.

No Room for Misunderstanding

Nevertheless, simplicity, alone, does not always provide instant understanding. Without a fine-honed organization of ideas, many words and phrases can play tricks on the unsuspecting mind.

The following notice was posted on a cruise ship belonging to a company in Ireland: "The chairs in the cabin are for the ladies. Gentlemen are requested not to make use of them until the ladies are seated."

Remember the lecturer who said: "Now pay close attention to the graph on the flip chart and I'll run through it."?

Such careless organization of ideas may be humorous at times, but frequently can have serious consequences.

Here is a message, albeit completely, concisely and simply worded, that is not immediately clear: "Turn left or get shot."

Even a small error or delay in understanding this sign posted in the riot-torn Watts district of Los Angeles might have been the last its readers could ever make.

Again we are reminded to write so that we cannot possibly be misunderstood. Write exactly what you mean and misunderstanding may be avoided.

For instance don't write, "He almost has enough

capital" when you mean "He has almost enough capital."

Nor could you improve corporate sales by writing: "The company only sells its products to customers within the state." Perhaps, you really meant: "The company sells its products only to customers within the state."

A misplaced phrase can cause serious distortion of meaning: "The attorney returned the contract that had been received in error by registered mail" is different in meaning from "The attorney returned by registered mail the contract that had been received in error."

A clear and vital development of an idea not only depends on *how much* but *how* a reader needs to be told in order to fully understand your meaning.

When a word or two slips into an unintended and improper position not only can the real meaning be diffused, but the sentence may be offensive.

"We hope you can *at least* send us $20 a month," is demeaning and, probably, unrewarding. Re-position the adverb: "We hope you can send us *at least* $20 each month."

Because we know clarity of purpose can be achieved by placing the most important idea in the most important position, we again call on punctuation. Pick the phrase you want to stress and frame it with commas. "I will prepare, *without obligation on your part*, a sketch of your trademark."

General Patton's critique of General Montgomery, "He is more concerned about not losing than about winning," is at first as mind-boggling as the sign in Watts. History made the meaning clear.

Similarly, George Romney, then Governor of Michigan, obliquely expressed this denial: "I didn't say that I didn't say it, I said that I didn't say that I said it."

Simple Sentences Are Successful

Rarely can readers be moved to action by a frothy compounding of several sentences. Lincoln would have said of such a writer: "He can compress the most words into the smallest ideas of any man I ever met."

Example: "I owe it to candor and the amicable relations existing between my company and yours to declare that we should consider any attempt on the part of our competitors to extend their operation within the boundaries of our mutual marketing areas as an indulgence we should not encourage."

Most of us would rather read (or write): "Should our competitors decide to move into this marketing area, I will certainly depend on your assistance to take necessary action."

Eliminating the excess verbiage and constructing a sentence with only related ideas makes the meaning immediately clear.

Each sentence should carry one major thought. Here is a compound sentence with unrelated ideas: "Thank you for the prompt report on your fire loss of July 18, and enclosed is a proof-of-loss form you need to initiate your claim" (clause not properly related).

"Thank you for the prompt report on your fire of July 18.

"Enclosed is a proof-of-loss form you need to initiate your claim."

Straight-Line Thinking

Copywriters and sales managers successfully impress us with an important idea by a device known as "emphasis by deliberate introduction": "Here is one certain way in which you can put a stop to the disappearance of expensive hand tools: Mark each one with your company name by means of an XYZ Engraving Tool."

(The same writer, however, might carelessly write: "Our sheer stockings are so serviceable, many women wear nothing else.")

In an opening statement, the clearly defined purpose will lead the reader (and the writer) into further discussion. Ideas cannot be organized clearly by a string of roughly connected thoughts in that statement.

CLOUDY: "We enclose the cancelled passbook for subject account, together with our check for the account in full, which she had ordered us to send to her before her death and which were returned to us by the Post Office Department because of her death."

CLEAR: (One idea for each sentence/paragraph) "We are sorry to learn of the death of Mrs. Jones, a valued customer.

"Here is the cancelled passbook and a check for the remainder of funds in her account.

"At Mrs. Jone's request, we had mailed them to her home, but the latter was returned by the Post Office."

The Topic Sentence and Theme

The topic sentence is the guideline. It either forecasts the main thought early in the paragraph or later summarizes the main thought.

Because of its general nature, a topic sentence, wherever placed, may require the support of other statements especially when specific information is needed.

Each paragraph in this letter holds a thought yet all the paragraphs are related and thus, coherent.

"Your suggestion for converting our old Widgets into saws appears to be practicable.

These Widgets, however, are not readily available, (gives the paragraph a start in unity). Our supervisors report that the only Widgets suitable for this purpose have been discarded and stored at various plants throughout the country. Because of the urgent need for saws, there is no time for conversion.

Our Ithaca, New York, plant needs 1,500 saws. (Follow with description of saws, if required.)

If you can fill this order, please let us know the price and date of shipment."

With the reader in mind, a topic sentence can be supported by using any one of these three methods: 1) Begin with the simple statement of an idea and end with its development; 2) Present the evidence and end with your interpretation of it; 3) Introduce your reasons in order of their credibility.

To do more than one at a time adds undesirable details that make long letters with short meanings:

Our supply of Widgets manufactured two years ago by XYZ Inc. has been depleted due to several large orders from companies in West Virginia and Maryland.

Therefore, we are sorry we cannot fill your order. If we had been able to, we would send along the promotional material you requested. Since we cannot ship the goods for another year, you will have no immediate use for this material until then, when it will be updated.

When ideas are organized in sequence, other devices may be used to strengthen thoughts.

For instance, bring out contrasts: "If we demand social justice, we must support community efforts"; "Labor costs are mounting, but the price of our product remains comparatively stationary"; and "The XYZ Metal Fence is sturdy in construction, yet light and easy to assemble."

A poor habit is to reinforce an idea by redundancy. Edwin Newman, author of *Strictly Speaking* and many other books on language usage, cites *singularly unique, spread of nuclear proliferation, very dormant, a mutual decision between us,* among the many inflated expressions to which many Americans are addicted.

Further, don't tack complex phrases on to the end of the sentence; it lends a trailing, let-down effect.

WEAK: "We have subjected our Model 724 to a series of the most exhaustive tests in order to prove the efficiency of its operation."

STRONG: "To prove the efficiency of its operation, we have subjected our Model 724 to a series of the most exhaustive tests."

Another device that expresses your idea more clearly and also increases interest is to place the topic clause first in a sentence or paragraph. Adverb clauses beginning with *when, if, as, since, although,* etc., tend to weaken the meaning when placed in first position.

For instance, *"Since it is important that we earn our fixed charges* by the end of the year, we must collect all past-due accounts within the next month,"* fails to stress the topic that is first in your thinking.

Transpose the first clause and you emphasize the important reason for the reader to take action: *"We must collect all past-due accounts within the next month...."*

It is not always possible to establish a topic sentence for each paragraph. In that event, a topic theme provides unity and coherence. The thread of the paragraph is followed easily because there is an association with the ideas in the other paragraphs. Thus the entire letter will be related to the topic theme.

The second paragraph of this letter contains the topic theme—an explanation of company policy:

Thank you for explaining that the ground formerly leased to you at Red Bank, N.J., is no longer being used and requesting that the lease be canceled.

Although the lease was originally issued to your company, it was later assigned to XYZ Inc. Therefore, our legal department suggests that a request for cancelation should originate with XYZ, Inc.

If you will direct the proper official of that company to send us such a request, arrangements for termination of the lease will begin at once.

Coherence Among Paragraphs

Usually, coherence among paragraphs is accomplished by three methods:

1) Personal pronouns are used to refer to an antecedent term in a preceding sentence, or thought connection between the sentences. "Your loan file does not show that *your taxes* have been paid for the past two years. No doubt you have paid them (your taxes), but please send us the receipts so that the information will be recorded in your account. They (the receipts) will be returned to you.

2) A common method of sustaining coherence between paragraphs is the repetition of a word or the use of a synonym:

It has been recommended that we continue to carry the *loan* until your company markets its new product in the spring.

As you know, the *loan* matures on June 1 of this year. (coherence through repetition of a word)

When the borrowers have signed the *extension agreement*, please return it to us. After this is executed on the part of our company, the document (extension agreement) will be returned to you.

3) Frequently, a transitional expression *looks back* to, or recalls, a sense of the whole idea:

The parcel containing 100 Widgets, which should have reached you several days ago, was misdirected. The order department will begin tracing it at once.

In the meantime, (while it is being traced) a

duplicate shipment was sent to you by express and should arrive by June 1.

Accentuate the Positive

A clear and vital development of an idea not only depends on *how much* but *how* a reader needs to be told in order to fully understand your meaning.

Also, a *positive* manner helps to achieve clarity and unity; any negative inference distracts the reader from either a topic sentence or a topic theme.

Even the most confident associate might find an unintended hint of your complete dissatisfaction when a memo reads: "This report never goes into any phase of the matter in detail, but covers each part too briefly."

In most circumstances, it is better to convey your idea in a more explicit and pleasant manner: "Thank you for the report, Bob. I certainly appreciate the time and effort in preparation, although more information about each phase would be most helpful."

To make a negative statement in a positive fashion avoid using *do not,* one of the most common implements of negativism. Write: "I believe continuance of the inquiry is a waste of time," instead of the weaker: "I do not think that continuing the inquiry is a reasonable way to utilize our time."

Words, like missiles, go farthest when they are smoothest.

For instance, here's a typical notice from thousands of corporations and businesses every day: "If you don't pay this installment by June 1, there will be an added penalty." Certainly, the idea is expressed with clarity and unity, but it not only knocks, but threatens. The reaction is tantamount to a slap in the face.

Negative expressions can pad sentences unnecessarily and usually sound obsequious. Example: "If the enclosed information is not sufficient and you feel you need more, kindly let me know."

Condensed in a positive manner, your idea is expressed clearly: "If you need more information, please let me know."

Avoid negatives such as "we fail to understand," "we are at a loss to know," "you neglected to state." These only lead to the reader's preoccupation with your oblique reference to his or her lack of good faith.

A collection letter, in particular, should also give the reader the benefit of the doubt. Generally, there are better results from letters that avoid the hard-hitting negative tone: "Perhaps you just forgot to mail us a check this month," or "When can we expect payment of . . .?" is more effective—at least on the first try.

In their manner of expressing ideas, many people go too far too fast with too little. Without full consideration for the topic and the possible reader reaction, it's easy to drop a word or construct a sentence that gives the impression of a slur where none was intended.

Executives do have the enviable reputation of being decisive, conclusive, diplomatic and—just human enough to show the strain of the constant pressure to connect thoughts with the proper symbols.

Such may have been the case when Gerald R. Ford, then the Chief Executive, wrote this memo to Garth Marston who was named acting chairman of the Federal Home Loan Bank Board:

"Would you kindly look after the savings and loan business until I can find someone capable of doing so?"

The former President's memo is displayed in Mr. Marston's office. He is a man of good humor.

Habit is a cable. We are threading it everyday, and at last we cannot break it.
— Horace Mann

6.

The Art of De-Sexing

Devices To Avoid Discrimination

Remember when a popular automobile advertisement urged us to "Ask the Man Who Owns One?"

It became a household slogan, a flippant answer to silly questions. And Buicks were bought, not boycotted. The means achieved the end, unhampered by firm objections to the masculine-oriented language from government agencies or powerful activist groups.

Today, not only do men and women share the buying power, but a large sector of a more sophisticated public would be rankled by such a statement. Business communicators have learned that this lead to red marks on balance sheets and smudges on corporate images.

Perhaps there would be more converts to the con-

cept of anti-discrimination if all of its proponents would
try to effect a diplomatic change in mind-sets simply by
"practicing what they preach." For instance, many admirable feminists who take their cause into legislative
halls then return to offices where sexist language is con-
doned by its usage.

The whole process is slow to infiltrate corporate and
bureaucratic strongholds, possibly because the methodology seems complex when it is not. To accomplish a
graceful transition, a knowledge of simple terminology
and various construction devices is essential.

De-sexing the language is not intended to be the sole
precinct of classified ad writers or personnel directors.
Non-sexist language should flow generally through letters, reports, memos, house organs, press releases,
literature, annual reports, etc.

The Justice Department is slowly getting the message. A task force delved into 4,000 federal laws to weed
out the discriminatory sex references affecting military,
Social Security and public assistance programs. On the
state levels, astute legislators are taking hard looks at
some sexist legalese.

Although business and industry moved quickly to
conform to rules concerning anti-discriminatory hiring
practice, there remains some reluctance to use other
methods of spreading the message of equality.

If for no other reason, the public's discontent with
chauvinistic expressions offers a fresh challenge to
sharpen the wits and join the parade.

Usually, it is the chief executive officer who sets the
pace for the language de-sexing process within the corporation. How many CEOs have issued directives which

advocate the control of sexist language in all corporate communication? How many have made a real effort to de-sex their own written statements whenever possible? According to a survey by the International Association of Business Communicators, cooperation is minimal.

Those on management level can be a viable force in altering the thought processes of many people by encouraging changes in terminology, construction and semantics.

De-Sexing Guidelines

This activity is more apparent in the publishing field than in the corporate arena. Editors and authors have been issued strong guidelines for the equal treatment of the sexes. Corporate management should "take a leaf from their book"; written business communications are no less influential than other non-fiction.

"Guidelines for Equal Treatment of the Sexes in McGraw-Hill Book Company Publications," is an 11-page policy statement based on the premise that "Men and women should be treated primarily as people, and not primarily as members of opposite sexes. Their shared humanity and common attributes should be stressed, not their gender difference. Neither sex should be stereotyped or primarily assigned to a leading or secondary role."

Segments of the "Guidelines" with special interest to business writers make the following points:

(A) Though many women will continue to choose traditional occupations, such as homemaker or secretary, women should not be typecast in these roles but shown in a wide variety of professions and trades: as doctors and dentists, not always as nurses; as principals and professors, not always as

teachers; as lawyers and judges, not always as
social workers; as bank presidents, not always as
tellers; as members of Congress, not always as
members of the League of Women Voters.

(B) Similarly, men should not be shown as constantly subject to the "manculine mystique" in
their interests, attitudes, or careers. They should
not be made to feel that their self-worth depends entirely upon their income level or the status level of
their jobs. They should not be conditioned to
believe that a man ought to earn more than a
woman or that he ought to be the sole support of a
family.

(C) An attempt should be made to break job
stereotypes for both women and men. No job should
be considered sex-typed, and it should never be implied that certain jobs are incompatible with a
woman's "femininity" or a man's "masculinity."
... Women within a profession should be shown at
all professional levels, including the top levels.
Women should be portrayed in positions of authority over men and over other women,and there should
be no implication that a man loses face or that a
woman faces difficulty if the employer or supervisor
is a woman."

Here are a few of McGraw-Hill's examples:

NO	*YES*
career girl or career woman	Name the woman's profession: attorney Ellen Smith; Marie Sanchez, a journalist *or* editor *or* business executive *or* doctor *or* lawyer *or* agent.

Jim Weiss allows his wife to work part-time.	Judy Weiss works part-time.
I've often heard supervisors say, "He's not the right man for the job," or "He lacks the qualifications for success."	Alternate male and female expressions and examples: I've often heard supervisors say, "She's not the right person for the job," or "He lacks the qualifications for success."
the secretary . . . she	secretaries . . . they
the breadwinner . . . his earnings	the breadwinner . . . his or her earnings *or* breadwinners . . . their earnings
Henry Harris is a shrewd lawyer and his wife, Ann, is a striking brunette.	"The Harrises are an attractive couple. Henry is a handsome blond and Ann is a striking brunette." or "The Harrises are highly respected in their fields. Ann is an accomplished musician and Henry is a shrewd lawyer." or "The Harrises are an interesting couple. Henry is a shrewd lawyer and Ann is very active in community affairs."

| *lady* used as a modifier, as in lady lawyer | lawyer (A woman may be identified simply through the choice of pronouns), as in: "The lawyer made her summation to the jury." Try to avoid gender modifiers altogether. When you must modify, use woman or female, as in: a course on women writers. |

Another (Better) Way To Say It

Business writers, in particular, are prone to use constructions that place either a man or woman in a special class. We should avoid emphasizing one gender over the other in an effort to portray his or her feat as extraordinary in view of his or her sex.

The modern executive, whatever the gender, should think twice before writing: "Though a man (or a woman), he (or she) runs the secretarial pool efficiently" or "I will instruct my *girl* to send the report to you."

"He (or she) runs the secretarial pool efficiently" and "I will instruct my *secretary* to . . ." is not likely to offend either the male or the female employee.

For the same reason, unbalanced stereotyping should be eliminated by equal treatment. For instance, this sentence is balanced by eliminating *female* since identification by sex is irrelevant: "Arthur Adams is one of our best supervisors and Nancy Nimble is one of the best managers."

Also, over-identification by repeated emphasis of gender is unnecessary as in "Messrs. Robert Jones and

James Smith, each man qualified in his field. . . ." The writer seemed determined to the make the point that maleness was essential to proficiency.

Stereotyping of the logical, objective male and the emotional, subjective female should be avoided. Therefore, Jane Jones, whenever relevant, should be described as a logical thinker, problem solver, or decision maker—qualities heretofore more frequently attributed to male executives.

Avoid constructions implying that women, because of their sex, are always dependent on male initiative. Example: "Our president, James Copeland, *allows* women to have considerable opportunity for advancement in our corporation." An alternative is: "Women have considerable opportunity for advancement in our corporation, according to our president."

Most stereotyped phrases that exude sexism have become extinct such as "woman's work" or "man-sized job."

Others have been replaced:

PASSÉ	*ACCEPTED*
the best man for the job	best person (or candidate) for the job
the common man the man on the street	ordinary people
the man who pays the property tax	the person (the one) who pays the property tax
the typical American . . . he	typical Americans . . . they
the motorist . . . he	motorists . . . they, the motorist . . . he or she

early man	early human, early men and women
when man invented the...	when people invented...
sweet young thing	young woman, girl
housewife	homemaker
grow to manhood	grow to adulthood
man made	of human origin, artificial, synthetic, manufactured
the distaff side, the fair sex, the weaker sex	the women
the better half, the little woman	wife

Clichés are easily corrected; more oblique expressions require harder treatment. For instance, the objectionable "gee whiz" attitude about men or women who perform competently is reflected in such statements as: "Though a woman, she ran the business effectively," or "Though a man, he is an excellent nurse."

A few male employers unwittingly use a patronizing tone by mentioning a woman's mental attributes only in second place to her physical qualities.

The female candidate for any position should not be described as "a pert brunette mother of three." In the white-collar world (a term which carries its own inference), the corporal attributes of a male applicant are rarely mentioned as a *primary* qualification, if at all.

Re-think Grammar

The swing to non-sexist writing often requires more than word changes; it is best effected by grammatical reconstruction of sentences.

Begin by taking a good look at a sentence in which you refer to a hypothetical person. Does it include a masculine or feminine pronoun? If so, you may be giving a gender to one who should be neutered in the best interest of non-sexist writing. More often, the pronoun is simply unnecessary.

Example: "A good boss is someone who takes a little more than *his* (her) share of the blame and a little less than *his* (her) share of the credit."

Substitute *a* for the pronoun(s) (more than *a* share—less than *a* share) and you de-sex the sentence without altering the meaning or resorting to *his or her.*

The use of *his or her* is awkward and usually unnecessary. "The average executive has difficulty composing *his or her* letters" should be reconstructed: "Composing letters is difficult for the average executive" or you may pluralize: "Most executives find it difficult to compose letters."

Only if there is a need for subtle reference to your company's beneficence would you write: "Our Vice President has placed your name on *her* mailing list," instead of "Your name has been placed on the mailing list by our Vice-President."

Fortunately, the English language has plural neuter pronouns. Try pluralization with *those, their* and *they*: "The *men* (*women*) in the accounting division are authorized to sign request forms."

Request forms should be signed by *those* in the accounting division.

Each employee has *his* own duties to perform.
As employees, *they* each have duties to perform.

In order for an employee to be promoted, *he* should receive an evaluation from *his* supervisor.
In order for employees to be promoted, *they* should receive evaluations from *their* supervisors.

Another technique is to establish first in the reader's mind that you are taking the preferred middle position at the outset regardless of the gender pronouns to follow.

John D. Glover and Gerald A. Simon, editors of the *Chief Executives' Handbook* published by Dow-Jones, Inc. (1976), show us how.

On the first page of the first chapter titled "The Many Roles of the Chief Executive," Dr. Glover of Harvard University firmly establishes the typical CEO as a person of either sex by such statements as "... he—or she—is supposed to know everything and to be everything" and "A man—or woman—for all seasons." After this explanation, *"he* or *she"* and *"a man* or *woman"* are freely used in references to CEOs made by the 91 executives who contributed to the 1,106-page compilation. The opening clarification tends to convince us that the subsequent masculine terms are not sexist, but generic. Thus, the writers are absolved of biased attitudes and the editing is made easier.

This approach may work equally well in the preparation of a long proposal or report, but is likely to add unnecessary explanatory verbiage to the shorter letter form. Under ordinary circumstances, it is better to choose alternative expressions rather than cling to the generic use of *he, him,* or *man* that may invite criticism.

The government's *Man*power Administration, however, continues to use a generic form while recommending to others that *human power, human energy, workers* or *workforce* are good substitutes for *man*power. Perhaps the bureaucrats view the term as broadly as the captain of a cruise ship who beguiles the passengers with the trivial report that "man overboard is now a navigational term."

Fortunately, the movement into greater awareness transcends the ridiculous into the sublime. Work is underway to revise much of the language in the Christian scriptures, the Koran, the Bhagavad-Gita and other religious writings. This, indeed, marks the seriousness of all-out efforts to eliminate sexist language.

Males Are Subjected to Discrimination, Too

The effort that may have brought the need closer to our attention probably began as early as 1890 when Susan B. Anthony addressed her followers as "My Fellow Countrywomen." Some men, today, would view this as an undesirable substitution for *man* in a well-known salutation.

The few who overwork the feminist view, and by so doing avoid the principle of equal treatment, rarely notice language that discriminates against males.

"Each teacher in the school district received *her* salary increase" is as objectionable to a male teacher as "We will consult an attorney and get *his* opinion" is to a female attorney. "... received *a* salary increase" and "... get *an* opinion" are adequate.

Also, in the event of a criminal action, it is generally

implied that the suspected culprit is a man. "Our records show an unexplained deficit that indicates a fraud has been perpetrated. The man responsible will be apprehended," is not only biased, but likely to be disproven. *Person* is suitable, only if there is not a specific substitute such as *accountant, employee,* etc.

Person-ification

Person has suffered from overuse by those who find it tiresome to practice other methods of de-sexing. Thus, the word has become subjected to good-humored ridicule.

Do not use *person* when there is a better choice. If it's part of an official title, however, you have no choice; learn to live with it! For instance, today a student at the Annapolis Naval Academy is a "midshipperson" and one who has completed Protestant seminary training is called a "clergy person."

To avoid the lumbering euphemism, *chairperson,* most parliamentarians have conceded that *chair* has been around for three centuries and is approved by the *Oxford English Dictionary* and other authorities as a preferred substitute for *chairman* or *chairwoman.*

Even more revered than dictionaries is the famous *Robert's Rules of Order* that advises presiding officers to address the meetings as "the chair" as in "The chair rules that. . . ." This should automatically neuter a title.

Nevertheless, it further states that the presiding officer should be addressed by his or her official title, as Mr. or Madame President. If there is no special title, or in a meeting of any organized body, the form "Mr. Chairman" or "Madame Chairman" should be used. (The latter title came into being when a woman first entered Congress in 1920.)

On the corporate level, the only way to avoid "He (she) is chairman of the board" is to write "He (she) chairs the board" or better: "The board of directors is chaired by Jane (John) Jones" or—as a title, John (Jane) Jones, not *chairman* or *chairwoman*.

Mr., Mrs., Ms. and the Like

The English language will not become what you and I want it to become, it will become what we *use*. Remember lady comes from "loafmaker" or "she who makes bread." This is a long way from its common use as a courtesy title that refers to a woman with fine manners. It should not be a reckless synonym for a female with less attributes.

For the same basic reason, *gentlemen* should not be arbitrarily substituted for *men*. Even today, it rightfully alludes only to those with good breeding and social standing. It should be reserved for this purpose lest it, too, becomes extinct. This is another reason why a letter's salutation, "Dear Gentlemen" should be avoided.

Also, primarily because of its overuse, *Mr.* is no longer regarded as a prestigious title nor does it carry a connotation from its derivative, *master*. It can be dropped easier than more meaningful titles such as *Senator, The Honorable, The Reverend*, etc.

It is because of *Master* that *Mistress* was devised. Eventually, the abbreviations of the feminine version, *Mrs.* or *Miss* were needed to clarify the marital state. Today's popular term, *Ms.* is considered to mean either married or unmarried.

Ms. arbitrarily used as a synonym for *Mrs.* may be

construed as a contrived and unnecessary means of flattery. Further, there are many who prefer *Mrs.*; when this preference is known, it should be used. Business and professional women generally prefer the use of their full names rather than either *Mrs., Miss* or *Ms.*

To avoid a hassle and save a few typing strokes, eliminate all titles. Most computer labeling machines dropped titles long ago. Remember, however, if there is any possibility that the absence of a title may offend any one with whom you communicate, include it. It's customer and employee relations that counts!

Job Titles

Occupational language has undergone drastic facelifting under the aegis of the Labor Department. Its *Dictionary of Occupational Titles* was a dozen years in the making, has 1,300 pages and weighs in at more than five pounds. The Fourth Edition (1979) is a codified compilation of jobs, ordinary and unusual.

Of special interest to business writers and members of public employment services is: "Job Title Revisions to Eliminate Sex-and-Age-Referent Language." This publication brings job titles listed in the *Dictionary* into conformance with equal employment legislation, and with recent administration policy statements and instructions on the same subject. Wherever possible, job titles have been revised in favor of titles that do not connote age or sex.

The most drastic obliteration is that of *man* as well as *woman* from job titles.

It will take some doing to refer to that obviously male or female person responsible for sales volume as a "sales associate," "sales agent," or "sales representative." Nevertheless, such well-worn sexist titles as *salesman* and *saleswomen* are being comfortably replaced.

We also refer to the watchman as *guard* and the furnace man as a *furnace tender*. The draftsman has become a *drafter;* the foreman a *supervisor;* a fireman, a *firer;* a repairman, *repairer;* serviceman, *servicer;* maintenance man, *maintainer;* yardman, *yard-worker;* charwoman, *charworker* and the mail comes by way of a *mail carrier* or *letter carrier.*

It is not too difficult to follow these patterns cut to fit anti-discrimination laws and popular philosophy when true awareness and methodology take a firm grip on your mind.

At times, these innovations may seem to be nonsense, but time-worn habits are easily changed when new language rules are observed.

They will have the greatest impact on the public when set into practice by our commercial leaders—those on the management levels of America's businesses and industries. In time, non-sexist language will be the rule, not the exception.

Corporate management may even enjoy its covenant to de-sex the language gracefully without the pressure of picket lines or the thumping of drums on Capitol Hill.

You may or may not agree with much that is expected of us, but you will find it challenging to play the game and—rewarding. As Damon Runyon wrote, "It may be that the race is not always for the swift, nor the battle to the strong—but, that's the way to bet."

Every letter is a self-portrait of the person who wrote it.

7.

The Great Dictators

And Those Who Aren't

Faced with the pressure of daily correspondence, some executives seem to undergo personality changes or indulge in a kind of role-playing. Temporarily, they become what they are not. Others reveal what they really are, or think they are, for better or worse.

During the dictation metamorphosis, the usually reserved person may flay the air-waves in a walnut-paneled kingdom to expound the latest edict in eloquent language.

Conversely, the CEO who regularly delivers straightforward verbal reports in simple language freezes at the sight of a recording machine or a pencil poised for shorthand.

And, of course, there are the many executives who have brilliant reputations for decision-making, yet delegate their writing responsibilities to associates whose best decision any day may be to go to work.

Every communication created during a dictation session becomes either a true and realistic self-portrait or one that is false and contrived.

As we look more closely at the various types of dictators, we should realize that many of their worst faults are shared by even the best of us.

The Rambler

The Rambler comes to the task unprepared and, most always, is unenthusiastic. He or she really doesn't know exactly what to say or how to say it, but pretends that all of it will be sound and reasonable.

If the Rambler's dictation cannot overwhelm with quality, it can overwhelm with quantity. Result: a letter long enough for the writer, but not short enough for the reader.

Lost in a mire of wordage, the Rambler recoups a thought and begins again. The problem, of course, is a lack of organization and a compulsion to keep the dictation going. A good secretary will wait while any dictator reaches for a word, a phrase or an idea.

But the need to wait would lessen if, prior to dictation, the Ramblers would ask themselves: What is the purpose of this letter? Is the back-up material at hand or familiar? What really needs to be said and what is the proper order?

The Rambler's sense of insecurity is reflected by the repeated use of the words "you know," stilted phrases such as "to be sure," and the seemingly endless "uh-uh-uh. . . ." These crutches and expressions of hesitancy slip out when there's nowhere to go, nothing better to say, and the Rambler wants to get it over with—somehow.

Until The Rambler takes the time to prepare and becomes more self-assured, drafting letters in longhand would be a sensible alternative. This gives an opportunity to weed out the clutter and organize ideas.

Many executives prefer this longhand method and many more secretaries would encourage it—if the handwriting were more legible.

Dictated letters, especially by Ramblers, may be time-eaters. Re-writing, editing, re-typing and sometimes, re-dictating may be required. Why go around twice when once would be enough? Be your own editor. Draft the letter in longhand or make copious notes and follow them while dictating.

The Erratic

The Erratic, rambling-wise, is a kindred soul but is more apt to wear out recorder switches and secretaries. At every lap of the track, the mind changes and sometimes even stops to shift gears.

The energy expended on "strike that" would have been better applied to brief meditation before speaking each sentence.

A survey among members of the National Secretaries Association, Delaware chapter, revealed the most disturbing habits of their bosses to be: "the constant changing of thoughts" and "dictation of just fragments."

One may be erratic in the throes of dictation only because of momentary stress. The Erratic needs to relax, to hold tight to the purpose of the communication, set up a firm preliminary plan, and resolve not to be distracted from without or within.

The Orator

The Orator's products are most likely to be lost in a "snow" storm rather than a literary fog. The Orator presents brilliant speeches applauded by captive audiences, but carries over the same type of high-sounding language into written communication where it is rarely appreciated.

As George Eliot wrote: "He was like a cock who thought the sun had risen to hear him crow."

Jargon springs forth as though pre-recorded. For example: "Without effective interface, coupled with substantive input, we cannot hope to have any definitive impact," or "The milieu of collaboration should be interfaced with parameters of priority for optimum bottom-line accountability."

It is interesting that one of the by-products of the current battle against business and bureaucratic gobbledygook has been the gobbledygook generated by those who prohibit it. For instance, a Delaware insurance commissioner decided to promulgate a regulation telling the insurance companies how to write readable policies. The statement: "Initiation of a readability project affords the insurer a unique opportunity to rearrange the contract into a logical thought outline-flow sequence."

Such is the way of oratorical-types who one day realize that such lengthy exposition is too tiring, too time-consuming and bores most readers.

Until then, we can hope that the least relevant portions of The Orator's dictation and the fancy phrases, however impressive, be excluded from the final draft by someone who isn't afraid to ask for permission to do so.

The Rapid-Fire Dictator

The company's chief language polluter often is the Rapid Fire dictator. At a speech rate far above the average, the process moves all too swiftly toward a breathless conclusion long-awaited by a suffering secretary.

Not only is the speech pattern staccato, but there's great dependence on verbal security blankets. Readily available terms such as "low profit," "spin-off," "in depth," "agreed in principle" and buzz-words like "stagflation" and "short fall" help to accelerate the speech.

The fertile mind of the loquacious Rapid-Fire dictator also stores a collection of one-sentence "form" explanations in answer to most any questions.

Here's one: "The financial statement reflects the unrealized appreciation (or—depreciation) of amounts in the participants' general and stock accounts section of the statement of trust assets and trust fund balances which represent the cumulative adjustment on company shares made to the records in order to record all of the assets at quoted market value."

All this and more comes so rapidly because the jargon is there and easily harvested. The greatest reward seems to be a kind of self-gratification when it can be delivered with a minimal time spent for breathing. Slow down and give yourself a chance to be original, correct and concise.

The Mumbler

The Mumbler may be a prime subject for that inevitable question, "What did you say?" Of course, there are many secretaries who have been coping for years and acquired an "ear" for jumbled monotones. They are exceptions. Generally, members of typing pools and relatively new secretaries are unaccustomed to The Mumbler's dictating style. This leads to inaccuracies or time-consuming, nerve-wracking explanations and repetition.

As speech therapists know, much indistinct speech comes from mouths on chins hung low, drowning the sound in neckties or scarves. High chin and eye contact will direct the voice to the proper source.

Some secretaries report that executive habits of stringing paper clips, smoking, filing nails, jangling keys, tapping fingers, twirling paperweights, pacing, paper-shuffling and staring out the window, usually go hand-in-hand with mumbling.

Poor articulation, more often caused by those momentary distractions, can also be traced to speech habits, resulting from locked jaw, lazy lips and/or the mushy mouth. Correcting the worst of these habits will lessen the possibility of distorted meanings. Further, good articulation is a joy to shorthand-writers and essential for machine dictation.

The Hedger

And then there's The Hedger who babbles and quibbles, hems and haws, stumbles and grumbles to avoid making a firm commitment about anything.

The Hedger performs as though each word is a signal for potential danger. Therefore, words weighed too carefully are apt to produce a cold and abrupt message.

The over-cautious Hedger invariably writes, rewrites and re-directs. Then the letters, memos and reports must be researched, analyzed, verified, encoded, translated, extrapolated, condensed and typed in triplicate!

In most instances, even the slightest hint of personal involvement in the matter discussed is avoided with or without a reason. Although the message carries The Hedger's signature, each inadvertent *I* is liable to be corrected to a *we*. Only when writing on behalf of your corporation or organization, should *we* and *us* be used and then—sparingly.

There's also added strain in dictation when the Hedger, avoids *you* as much as possible. "The report must accompany the proposal," translated into more friendly businessese should read: "When you submit your proposal, please include your report."

The Hedger believes there's less chance of being sued or "involved" if the passive or "nobody" voice is used. The anonymity is a device to create the World's Dullest Writing. In the passive voice, subjects do not act; they are acted upon.

Some of the cold, lifeless, evasive expressions are "it was necessary," "it was suggested," "it was recommended" or broad statements such as "An investigation is being made."

The experienced Hedger also is well-versed in the "pass the buck" technique, although it may not always be necessary. Because of explanatory comments designed to relieve executive responsibility, another five minutes is added to dictation time. Example:

Because of the inadvertence of one of our clerks you were notified on April 1 that there were not sufficient funds in your account.

It will be appreciated that the large volume of work with which the bank is confronted, and the current personnel shortage render it virtually impossible to eliminate small errors of this nature, particularly those originating because of a similarity in names.

With all these modifications, communications grow longer, the dictator and the secretary become weary of mental gymnastics and, the cost of the letter skyrockets in terms of time and labor.

A few *Super*-Hedgers never get that far; they never go at all. When confronted with "problem letters," they opt to ignore them on the premise that most any matter will resolve itself. At times, this is true, as any good executive knows. To the Super-Hedger, it means one less letter to dictate. Unfortunately, there also may be one more dissatisfied customer or client.

On the corporate level, there are, of course, occasions when this extraordinary talent for hedging may be useful. Mostly, it is a habit that stems from the dictator's concern that readers may be foes rather than friends.

The habit of hedging could be corrected if the dictator could use a more friendly attitude and a casual style of writing. When dictating, speak to the reader in the same relaxed and trusting manner as one would with most persons seated across the desk.

The Good Guys/Gals

The Amiable, for instance, dictates in a warm, approachable, and cooperative manner and produces clear and concise letters that create good will.

The Analytical has few signs of nervousness, possesses controlled body movement and speaks slowly about things, ideas, facts, while using time to be accurate and build credibility.

The Driver is eager to communicate each point, speaks quickly but with measured comments, and is primarily interested in establishing rapport with the recipient of each letter or memo.

The Expressive executive uses grimaces and body movements for emphasis not readily noticed by a busy shorthand writer and completely wasted on a tape recorder or dictaphone. The Expressive tends to be impulsive; the secretary must be geared to rapid change. The thrust of the Expressive's letter is to stimulate reader reaction and action—and it usually does!

The Delegators

In a class by themselves, are those who could be dictators, but prefer to be Delegators.

There are two types of Delegators. Neither one dictates nor drafts, but reserves the time and energy for other demanding, and, in some cases, more interesting executive obligations.

Delegator I is an accomplished business writer but, as a top executive, increases productivity by assigning well-trained secretaries, correspondents, administrative assistants, or an entire Public Relations department to compose his or her executive communication. This delegation is essential only insofar as no single person could cope with a large corporation's heavy volume of correspondence.

Nevertheless, the writers know that Delegator I has the knowledge to evaluate their efforts and assumes responsibility for the effect of each piece of written material by affixing a signature that implies it is his or her own work.

Delegator II, however, is one of many executives for whom delegation is an easy out of what appears to be a hard task.

This person rarely goes beyond stamping incoming letters with a "Yes," "No," or "Maybe," rather than draft or dictate responses. The reasons for the reluctance usually are no more than a lack of enthusiasm and a weak command of the language.

Fortunately, there are qualified business writers in the company to do the job. Yet, Delegator II is equally responsible for each word albeit written by someone else.

This executive, even as those who write, can do little more than scan the finished product with a single purpose in mind: search for typing and spelling errors. As you know, there is more to consider. Yet, the ability to catch such errors is no less important.

The state of language in America should be another deterrent to encouraging complete dependency on others. Good corporate writers may be members of an endangered species. Replacements are becoming increasingly difficult to find. Many academic English courses focus on literature—not grammar, spelling, and word usage. And there are too few who are knowledgeable about the techniques and forms of business writing.

Guidelines for Great Dictators

The Great Dictators throughout corporate America are the executives who:

1) Marshall facts and figures, establish the gist of their messages and plan construction prior to dictation.

2) Make an effort to prevent unnecessary interruptions during a dictation period.

3) Indicate clearly the type of communication: a letter, memo or a report; how many copies are needed, and if it is to be rushed.

4) Think each sentence through before dictating it and move smoothly from one paragraph to another coherently.

5) Relax and then speak smoothly without undue hesitation and at a pace comfortable for the transcriber.

6) Articulate each word clearly and pronounce words correctly.

7) Dictate directly to secretaries or recorders and control personal mannerisms that may be distracting.

8) Use a friendly tone as though the reader is seated on the other side of the desk.

9) Avoid repeating the message of the incoming letter and other needless verbiage.

10) Get to the point or purpose in the opening paragraph, always with the reader in mind.

11) Control bombastic language, oratorical tones, gesticulation, and repetition of words and phrases.

12) Articulate words and give added voice emphasis to phrases which may be unfamiliar to the transcriber or easily misinterpreted.

13) Spell unusual words and proper names and dictate figures carefully.

14) Do not permit a request for repetition of a dictated sentence or word to distract their thought patterns.

15) Have the message read or played back to make certain it is as dictated.

16) Ask for a rough draft when changes are anticipated.

17) Assume the blame for any errors that were made as a result of faulty dictation.

18) Mark minor corrections in such a way (with pencil or marginal notes) that the material does not need to be re-typed.

19) Compliment secretaries for accurate transcriptions, well prepared letters, memos, reports, and whatever auxiliary help was needed.

20) Give the best advice: Be yourself.

The strongest memory is weaker than the palest ink.

8.

Memos and Other Miseries

Breaking the Bafflegab Barrier

If memos were abolished, the fountains of industry might choke and most streams of in-house communication dry up. Yet, as *Business Week* reports, "Many supervisors, managers, scientists and otherwise bright executives cannot produce a clearly written, logically organized inter-office memo... and often do not realize it."

Write a Memo When....

Basically, the trouble stems from an overuse and misuse of the memorandum style as a format for all types of messages. One should write a memo only when the subject matter does not require the structure of a letter or a report. The memo is a report, in a sense, but should only be used for informal communication in as few words as possible. To do otherwise, would cause overly-long corporate memos noted for their roundabout approach, excess wordage and needless information. Because of a memo's friendly and informal tone, and because "it's only a memo," the writer foregoes the advantage of organization offered by the structure of a report.

Memo-writers often try to hit the target by using all their ammunition without careful aim. Pet circumlocutions and bombastic expressions in a message from the top are not always understood or appreciated by the troops. A single memo can affect many persons and projects throughout a department, within the entire corporation, a plant or a subsidiary—all in one fell swoop.

This is the big difference between a memo and a letter. A letter may reach only *one* person; a widely distributed memo will reach persons of different educational backgrounds and interests.

The Meat of the Memo

Would the language in this memo motivate even your most learned employee to "turn down the heat"?

Due to the diverse modulation of severity in the seasonal elements, we propose the limited curtailment of the plenitudinous exercitation of fuels by submitting the thermostats to drastic change wherever such action is feasible.

Conversely, the effectiveness of inter-office memos can be weakened by a casual, hasty, slangy presentation of a company policy or a directive that deserves more

dignified language. If the subject does not; the reader
does. The one-big-happy-family image may have its own
merits, but it is no excuse for devoting less time and
talents to writing a memo for employees than you would
for a consumer letter.

Especially in large companies where personal contact with management is less likely, employees may
superficially judge their superiors by the quality and
tone of management memos. A memo that is friendly
but insistent, considerate but constructive, or sympathetic yet firm (and in as few words as possible) is best
appreciated.

Memoranda that serve to avoid belly-to-belly con-
frontations are packed with high-powered verbal ammunition. In the heat of anger, one should pause to
remember the permanancy of written communication.

Although Robert Townsend, in his book, *Up the
Organization* maintains that "Murder-by-Memo is an acceptable crime in large organizations . . .", most compe-
tent managers prefer to settle such matters by telephone
or face-to-face.

Nevertheless, if the oral confrontation carries a risk
of misunderstanding and little validity for future
reference, then calmly compose a tactful memo as a
reminder and reinforcement of your particular view-
point.

Is every memo-trip necessary? Again, a brief phone
call or a short visit to or from a peer or group may be a
better means of quick communication.

Executives often decide that a series of memos could
replace the need for a meeting. "Three out of four executives have strong, negative feelings about meetings"

and feel they are "a waste of time, too long, dull, disorganized, inefficient, etc.," according to a study reported in *The Harvard Business Review*.

Some administrators write long memos, many with characteristics similar to the dullest of meetings. Although headed memo-style with *To, From, Date* and *Subject,* they tend to cover several subjects and a variety of intentions similar to a meeting agenda. Such an assortment of discussion topics is rarely presented effectively as a simple, informal memo.

Five Reasons for a Memo

Memos should *remind, inform, instruct, persuade* or *evaluate*. If there is a need to do more than one or two of these at the same time, write an informal report. Choose one intention for each memo.

Remind: The most common and most appropriate use of the memo form is as a reminder. You tell the readers what they should have remembered and may have forgotten or you add new information or correct a previous statement such as "The meeting scheduled for July 1 at 3 P.M. has been changed to July 3 at 2 P.M."

Inform: Readers are *informed only* when you tell them something they don't already know. This is an important memo because information is the chart and compass of business success. Don't lessen its impact by a clutter of other purposes.

To help your language conform to its intention 1) you must know what the reader(s) already knows, 2) make new information fully and unmistakably clear, 3) be sure the information is relevant to the interest and need(s) of the person(s) to whom the memo is directed.

Your sole objective is to put useful information into hands that can put it to work for you. Nothing more.

There's a great temptation to send copies of this well-written, organized, factual, Information Memo to everyone in the company, including those who really have no need for this information. Weed the distribution list; a memo that is unrelated to one's particular concern is perplexing.

Instruct: The memo that instructs differs from one that informs, not only because of its subject matter. It should contain some language that provides a psychological prod to follow the instructions.

Too many memos set forth instructions on *how* to do a specific job or implement a plan, but fail to present the reason(s) *why* it should be done or the mutual benefits expected. Although you are not running an educational institution, a verbalized understanding of exactly *what* you want done, *when, why* and *how,* builds efficiency.

Persuasive: Too many *persuasive* memos try to cover more than one situation.

Rarely can a single memo improve the morale of an entire company or resolve a company-wide problem that affects different people in different ways. Usually, such specific situations require more positive and personal action by top management.

Persuasion-by-memo is most effective in a practical sense such as motivating a sales force by a series of memos that compliment their efforts while urging an increase in sales by a certain date. Or—if directed to the personnel administration, for instance, a persuasive memo could cite the advantage of replacing a supervisor or hiring two receptionists instead of one.

Being specific about the immediate situation is especially effective when you want to change the reader's point of view. If you're sure the changes will not disturb balances in your organization, then commit your firm convictions as tactfully and concisely as possible. If your writing rambles, however, you may raise changes, objectives and negatives that are not really obvious.

If a long, building job of persuasion is needed for a particular situation or a rigid, fearful person needs to be moved step by factual step, don't depend on the short-form memo. Persuade in person and/or by letter, or incorporate persuasive language into a report or proposal.

Evaluation: A memo can be used to evaluate a business matter, but only when your facts and insights are equally well known to the reader and do not require repetition.

This type of memo should express confirmation or objection to a plan or opinion and give a generalized explanation.

If it is a complicated matter, in itself as well as in relationship to your business success, presentation in *report* form will give the subject more authority—and space.

Why Are Memos Necessary?

Memoranda may be just as fast or faster than personal calls or visits. The recipient has more time to prepare a fuller response. They may be less embarrassing than a verbal directive. In terms of time and value, they're probably cheaper than telephone calls. You can specify clearly your concerns in this short message. Memos create permanent records useful in future exchanges. Interdepartmental memos provide a history of actions and interactions.

Of special importance to you is the role memoranda play in satisfying executive hunger for valid information. As you know, in a constantly shifting business situation, those high on organizational charts do not always have a grasp of a particular aspect. Memos often provide the full overview that is needed for decision-making.

Pre-printed Forms

To be assured of immediate and brief information, the pre-printed memo form may be helpful. The single sheet with a tear-off would include your request and the response as well as a carbon copy for filing.

Memo-letter forms make an effort to combine the propriety of a letter with the brevity of a memo. Similar to other forms, it's available in two- or three-part sets that provide the original and file copies.

Generally, the memo-letter is distinguished from memo forms only by custom imprinting, if desired, that may be similar in appearance to a company's standard letterheads. Primarily, this form is used for speed and convenience.

Although these forms are widely used, they are not effective for all communication. Their convenience tends to encourage careless language and illegible scribbling.

Memo-writing will hit an all-time low if the "paper airplane office memos" gain popularity. These imprinted memo sheets fold up into a model of the Concorde and can zoom right to the boss's desk! It's a trip not likely to be enjoyed by executives intolerant of over-familiarity.

Memos to the Outside

Memoranda do take trips outside corporate walls, albeit not by "air mail." Again, they are on executive errands to ask or give a point of information.

Instead of a long letter that requires elaboration of the answer or request, the memo states its purpose and little else.

The curtness that would not be acceptable as letter-language, is not as objectionable in memo form. For instance, a memo sent to your peer in a friendly company might read: "What is the model number of the latest equipment required to accelerate production of Wonder Widgets?" The reply could be as brief as: "Model #240."

Manuals, Meetings and Media

No managerial action is complete unless there is a plan for communicating it. For this, we have manuals, meetings and media intended to have a positive effect, within corporate walls, on productivity.

In the wake of rising costs, administrators are re-evaluating the efficiency of these communication tools, as well as others.

For instance, too many employee manuals are padded by overblown language funneled into hundreds of pages, numerically indexed, and housed in expensive binders. As a less expensive alternative that meets employee needs, many companies are producing smaller manuals, each covering a separate topic. These concisely worded formats encourage a better understanding of procedures and policies and compel interest because they are less tiresome to read.

Little or no literary skill is required to prepare an agenda for a specialized meeting; its value can only be weakened by the addition of an inefficient statement setting forth the problem(s) or issue(s) to be discussed. When endless discussion is to be avoided, a concise and accurate statement of purpose for the agenda is more likely to inspire a coherent, thoroughly considered solution.

The medium you use for internal communication is most profitable when it meets the needs of persons downward in your corporation. Instructions regarding their work is an important need, but the need for motivation can be satisfied by the medium that gives employees a sense of teamwork and rapport with management.

A good house organ or newsletter serves both purposes, provided its information reaches the readers as "news" and not stale confirmation of "grapevine" rumors.

Unlike the operational manual or memo-directive, the newsletter offers a two-way mirror. It reflects a view of organizational behavior to management and, for each individual in the work force, a clearer picture of management concern and objectives.

In many companies, it may be the only means by which the CEO and others in the upper echelon can communicate more fully and directly with those whose respect, acceptance and understanding are vital to the profit structure.

Other media for corporate communication include press releases, annual reports, etc. The writing of these is best left to the professional business communicators and public relations specialists.

The Informal Report/Memo

When further comments or statistical data as back-up material is required, you would probably prefer to write or receive an Informal Business Report. It may be written in a casual memo style, but presented in the form of a report. Since it is assumed this report would also go to a committee, board or other persons for evaluation, it would be dignified by a heading:

XYZ Company

Personnel Changes
as of July 1, 1979

Submitted to the
Executive Committee
by
J. J. Jones,
Personnel Director

This short, informal report may have been solicited. If so, it would begin with one sentence or paragraph. For instance: "Here is the data you requested for a study of the methods for marketing our new product." Then, give the information. Don't report on the difficulties in obtaining the data or comment on the project's feasibility or include any information that has not been requested.

Unsolicited informal reports project ideas and plans you believe are worthy of consideration. They are less demanding of researchers than a formal report. Nevertheless, the essentials of effective writing are the same. Informal reports are written with a continuous-flow approach and personal style—a kind of glorified memo.

There's nothing wrong with writing this type of informal report in the first person; you are the rightful author. It was your initial outline, well prepared and polished, that gave birth to a fine report setting forth your view of a subject that may benefit the company.

By using your rough outline as a guideline, you can summarize your idea and its proposed implementation and, possibly, mention any change it may effect. You briefly mention cost factors, if feasible, and concisely analyze the situation that provoked the plan. All this can be done in the opening. You've made your best points right at the onset! Generally, further elaboration or back-up material is unnecessary at this stage.

Progress Reports

When weekly or monthly reports are expected from sales representatives, insurance adjusters, etc., printed report forms are practical because they insure uniformity. Further, no special writing expertise is required to answer the stated questions.

Although the format and details must be adapted to specific needs, most are simply headed:

Representative_____   WEEKLY SALES REPORT
                                 Week Ended_____
                                 Travel Expense_____

This is followed by questions such as "How many dealers did you call on?_____ and "Total products sold_____," etc.

Prepared report forms that list questions pertaining to internal operations are widely used in government and private industry. This method is a convenience to the person who has to fill them out and also the means by which companies can easily determine the facts. The limited space for answers encourages specific information, concisely written, rather than the lengthy, bureaucratic language of conventional reports.

Another kind of progress report chronicles the work that would solve a certain problem.

For this reason, great emphasis is placed on brevity. The reader wants to know what the report is about, what precisely has been done during a specific period, and what the plans are for the immediate future.

To provide this information, three simple subtitles form the pattern of organization: Statement of the Problem, Current Progress, Future Work.

The introduction may summarize earlier progress as background for the current report or simply bridge the gap between reports. Some progress report writers find the opening a good place for a brief statement of the conclusions reached and, if appropriate, their recommendations.

Most progress reports are organized topically; although some chronologically, with subtitles covering parts of the over-all period.

As for all reports, the main section should grow logically out of the subject matter and the requirements of those who want the report.

If data is required and it cannot fit comfortably into a sentence-paragraph pattern, add an Appendix to the report. Use your writing skill in the body of the report to evaluate and interpret remarks about the data presented at the end of the report.

The conclusion should be "prophetic." Reveal, insofar as possible, what you expect the coverage or scope will be in the next report. Be brief, use simple terminology and—don't promise too much. As you know, progress has not always measured up to predictions.

The Conventional "Full Dress" Report

Any report is usually viewed as a "print-out" of the input of one or more persons. In the case of a full formal report, the real author(s) may be mentioned, but rarely remembered; ultimately it becomes the work of a corporation.

The formal report could never be misunderstood for a memorandum or even an informal report. It has an impressive cover with a printed heading that names the company and the division, and the title, report number, and date. It carries an inside title page with the name(s) of the person(s) or company that prepared the report.

Space can also be provided for the signatures of those who approve, check and, if necessary, revise the report. There's also an area for "Remarks."

Generally, there is a transmittal letter immediately after the title page although you may prefer to mail or deliver this letter separately. Instead of a transmittal letter, you may want to write a Foreword which also introduces the report.

A Table of Contents comes next. Usually, it is an analytical outline modified in form for the sake of appearance. The majority of business report writers retain all the conventional outline symbols, i.e., capital letters and arabic numbers. Others produce a neater page by using indentation alone to show subordination. Either way, don't use minute subdivisions in the Table of Contents; three levels are usually enough.

If a report contains a half-dozen or more illustrations, (drawings, exhibits and the like) a List of Figures that gives the title and page number should follow the Table of Contents.

The body of the report then begins with a double-spaced, brief explanation of what is to come. Essentially, this is a Summary, although it may be called a Digest or Epitome.

Here is where your knowledge of correct and complete writing will shine. If someone else prepared the report, you will be better able to judge its effectiveness because of your own familiarity with what constitutes a good report.

Check the introduction carefully. It should give an overview of the essentials. Trouble will develop here if there is any possibility of misunderstanding because of a choice of words or because a sentence does not convey the intended meaning.

All reports seem to extend themselves into a special locution. Terms that are not accurate or explicit invite a time-consuming probe for exact meaning. For example, words like *connected, fastened* or *attached,* although not wrong in themselves, should not be used to denote the nature of a connection. Use *welded, soldered,* or *bolted.* Reports are expected to contain accurate and factual information rather than generalities or loose descriptive material.

As Mark Twain said: "The difference between the right word and the almost right word is the difference between lightning and the lightning bug."

Thorough thinking and careful expression are hallmarks of good formal report writing. As an example:

This report is based on a study of solar heating for homes. It is determined that the average lay person is concerned with the glare from the use of large areas of glass, yet *just the reverse* has been found to be true. Large windows, while admitting more usable light, *produce less* than several small openings.

Just the *reverse of* what? Produce *less* what?

Some believe that the longer the report; the greater the impression it will make. Perhaps that is why the federal government sent forth 11,400 words to report on California-grown olives and another 6,900 words dealing with peaches in Colorado.

Generally, reports should be made brief to ensure more successful cooperation and readability. It is difficult to find a short meaning in a long report!

The pitfalls and threats to shortness in letter-writing are much the same as for other report-writers with one exception: formal reports tend to use more abstract words.

Nature, character, condition, situation, etc., are corporate favorites. Also consider this: "The device is not one of a satisfactory description." *Description* is a useless appendage. Better: "The device is not satisfactory."

Excess wordage, too, seems to proclaim the special nature of the corporate report: Wordy: "An easy example for explanation purposes, etc., would be a shunt-wound motor." Better: "A shunt-wound motor is a good example."

Reports can be unclear when words are not used with concrete reference. "The new machine proved to be comparatively efficient," is not meaningful unless we know the efficiency of the machines with which the comparison is made.

And what is a "periodic interval"? A well-researched, careful report would state the time. Similarly, "a substantial increase in production" means little without specific amounts.

Some other words, dear to report writers, mean little or nothing for the purpose of thorough reporting. Here are a few:

appreciable	evident
reasonable	negligible
approximate	excessive
relative	suitable
considerable	fair
sufficient	undue

Redundant phrases run rampant through formal reports. Here are a few and their simple substitutes:

absolutely essential (essential)
actual experience (experience)
make application to (apply)
make contact with (see, meet)
completely eliminated (eliminated)
maintain cost control (control cost)
involve the necessity of (necessitates, requires)
prepare a job analysis (analyze a job)
provide a continuous indication of (continuously
   indicate)
subsequent to (after)
until such a time as (until)
with the object of (to)

All these report-writing mannerisms may be the reason you find most reports too long to be read comfortably and too ineffective for much of the same reason.

Your company may employ writing specialists or professional companies to prepare in-depth reports. Nevertheless, *you* must evaluate the finished report that bears your name and/or the name of your company.

The person who has verbalized your concept, idea or solution will only *share* the credit or blame. It is your focus that has provided the guiding light during the preparation.

Focus Is Essential

Focus is lacking in many company reports, especially those designed to be problem-solvers. There is a tendency to reiterate all the complexities rather than focus on the essential point(s). Two major actions are needed: define the problem and offer the solution.

Before the report is written, it is important to determine what information is needed and what levels of understanding must be reached. The specialist, casual observer, the CEO, etc., probably have different viewpoints. Because there are several personalities on the management level, there should be just enough information to satisfy all probable types of readers and still keep the picture in focus.

Another familiar factor to contend with is the influence of management's real or supposed desires on the writer. This type of pressure often distorts the focus.

Does the report present a solution that will be *acceptable,* rather than the best solution? If so, here is where some reports go wrong. Objective report writers operate on the principle that the *best* is always the *acceptable.*

Recommendation Reports

The only writing problems that may be new to you are how to phrase the recommendations and where to put them.

Tone, manner and emphasis are important; more so when you expect opposition to the recommendations you are convinced should be made. If this is anticipated, don't fall into an argumentative tone.

A report that begins with: "This is a very important report," may invite dispute or a suspicion that the report isn't too useful or important.

A good clear, statement that provides a reason for its importance is more effective. Example: "The great importance of this plan arises from the fact that. . . ."

In general, be forthright, but not blunt. Instead of writing, "The present system is inefficient and costly," (its developer may be on the review committee) take a more constructive approach: "The proposed new system is more efficient than the present method, and at lower cost because of the following factors . . ."

If you do not expect opposition, there is little problem in putting emphasis on the proper points, provided the logic of the situation is presented clearly.

Opposition, of course, is always probable. Play it safe; consider the probable attitude of the reader, and then discuss the advantages and disadvantages you think might be preferred. Then, present the course of action you intend to take. This way, emphasis is in the proper perspective.

When there is a need to make several recommendations, the style should be more formal and the material placed in logical organization.

Each main clause is presented in a list of complete sentences preceded by a subhead such as "Recommendation I." More often a simple introductory sentence, such as, "After consideration of all the information available, it is recommended. . ." can precede a list. For further emphasis, each recommendation could be accompanied by an explanatory sentence or two.

If the report is long, the recommendation(s) should be placed near the beginning, usually following the introduction so that the reader may at once find the major conclusions. In this case, the statement at the end of the report simply echoes the meaning, but in less formal language. It's a good device to make a lasting impression on the reader's mind.

The Proposal

As you know, a good proposal can mean money in the bank. It is commonly referred to as either solicited or unsolicited. The proposal can be written in response to an invitation to bid. An unsolicited proposal can present an idea or a plan to a prospective customer. Either or both can result in a sale or a contract.

Because every proposal is a special problem, it requires a special solution not only in technical content, but also in technique of presentation. Each one should be tailor-made, not an ill-fitting, ready-made job. That is why the writing of a proposal requires an extra effort to make words say exactly what you want them to say.

Don't give the reader anything more than is expected—language-wise. For instance, a purely perfunctory, stereotyped statement to the effect that "This is a proposal to..." is unnecessary. The reader has already seen the title page that identified the document.

A good introduction begins with an indication of your company's understanding of the invitation to bid or your proposal to do or build something, and a digest of the proposed solution or offer. The opening should close with a simple statement of the points to be covered in the remaining sections.

By all means, avoid overloading any proposal with a lot of "boilerplate" in which the reader has no interest. The proposal's quality will depend on how well you assembled all the information you present in writing. Is it adequate to sell the proposal?

It's also wise to do a preliminary study of activities which are not directly a part of the preparation, but make an indirect contribution. This will influence the style, strategy and organization of the proposal.

Too many proposals reflect a lack of thorough understanding of the customer's problems, the reasons for the invitation to bid, the required specifications. An analysis of the competition is helpful, too. All this will lead you into a wise choice of the points to be stressed and developed fully. You will then have the most effective order of presentation.

Again, an outline will serve as a convenient prod to your memory during the writing process. It should never be so binding, however, as to prevent you from using new ideas while you're making the first draft.

In the final draft, the formal outline serves as a Table of Contents. Remember that each heading should do its share of the work; say something more to the reader than "Look below."

Go over the text carefully. Proposal writing that is reader-proof will bring better results. Don't *assume* the words accurately portray your thoughts. It's a risk because at some stage, we may not actually *see* the words, but rather the facts and ideas which they intend to express. Will the words accurately express the same ideas to the reader as they do to you? It is often wise to have someone else read your copy before submitting the proposal. Of course, you will remember that highly technical terms, shop-talk, etc., may be unfamiliar to at least one of the proposal's several readers.

Also, select only those illustrations and figures that support your text. Don't embellish this proposal (or any report) with needless "window-dressing."

In some cases, a segment of a proposal may take exception to certain specifications. Phrase the exception so that it will not sound offensive or damage the proposal. Usually it can be done by giving a reasonable explanation for the exception and making clear that change is recommended in order to give a better product or service. In general, do not emphatically state that you cannot meet the requirements or specifications as requested; let the facts do it.

Save your most emphatic language for a conclusion designed to convince the customer that your company can produce. Repeat the solidly concrete features and selling points in simple, declarative sentences.

Avoid glib assurances, however, that your company is eager to be awarded the contract, etc. The reader is interested only in whether or not your company *can* produce.

If a proposal has been written by several authors, the need to weed out redundancies will probably be greater. Also check the information; sketchily-treated sections may need to be amplified in line with your own thinking.

When it reaches your desk, you will also know if the proposal is as customer-oriented as it should be. Does the introduction attract the serious attention of the reader—or lose it.? Does the writing style make a strong and favorable impression? Did the making of the proposal follow a time schedule that allows for the demands on your time and also enough time for administrative and service functions?

If it doesn't; send it back! It simply does not make sense to spend money and time to plan a good program and then dash off an inefficient manuscript intended to sell that program.

And selling is the name of the communication game. Whatever the medium, you sell your ideas, your products or services, your company and—yourself, directly or indirectly.

As Robert Louis Stevenson wrote: "Everybody lives by selling something." All our lives we work at the business of selling. Knowing the techniques and values of selling by letter, memorandum, report or proposal makes it easier—and no less exciting.

Make the reader say "that's true" at least three times. Sell fast with fast-selling sentences.

9.

Each to Its Own

For Every Purpose a Letter

Each letter does its own job best each in its own way. It should be designed either to inquire, request, acknowledge, order, complain, adjust, grant or refuse, collect, buy *or* sell.

All letters have in common the characteristics of courtesy and brevity and, generally, conform to the same pattern. All letters, in a sense, are sales letters. What, then, is the major factor, from a business point of view, that influences the differences among the various types of letters?

For best results, it is the writer's *attitude* that determines the appropriate tone and style. When *attitude* is in harmony with the purpose of each letter, it also serves as a guideline for a specific pattern of organization. An attitude that does not match the purpose encourages a dull uniformity that endangers a letter's personal effectiveness and suitable approach.

The Sales Letter

A letter intended to produce a sale is a prime example of how *attitude* can be projected to bring results—an attitude that stands for enthusiasm!

Enthusiasm is contagious; it engenders energy; reflects knowledge, and is the outward reflection of inner and corporate beliefs. As Emerson wrote: "Nothing great was ever achieved without enthusiasm."

Further, the enthusiastic participation of an executive, either as a writer or one who directs the effort, carries clout; it sells! Yet the process of selling by letter generally is avoided by those in top management who regard it as a highly specialized technique too demanding of executive time and energy. This need not be.

Most executives are a step ahead of some sales representatives, especially those garnered from outside sources to produce good sales letters or full promotions. An executive's relationship with the public has already been cemented by a multitude of administrative acts, including the writing of effective letters. And, of course, you have proven your confidence in the company and its products by sustaining an enthusiasm that is so easily reflected in writing.

It is only some confusion about the words and ways to sell that can depress natural enthusiasm and thus lead the executive away from trying to write a sales letter. All that is needed, assuming the material is there, is a workable formula applied in order of logical use.

And so we borrow a pattern from the advertising world: ADCA to create Attention, Desire, Conviction and Action.

Garnished with ideas that appeal and persuade, ADCA structures the message and helps the language flow freely for one single purpose: sell a product or service.

Begin with directing attention (A). With much the same motive as spinning flags at a gas station, the device may be a short but significant idea. And, of course, use the You Approach.

Questions are common openers, but should be used with caution lest reader interest ends before it begins. For instance, "Have you heard about our product?" signals the reader to mentally give a quick yes or no and then forget about the body of the letter.

"What have you read about our product?" is thought-provoking in a constructive sense. The reader is more apt to move forward into the message, impressed that you cared enough to ask.

Also, few readers are tolerant of a two-point question such as "You have $100,000 and you're considering investing as well as saving?" This may prompt the reader to mentally scream "decisions, decisions!" before being convinced to make one. Never distract attention by too much, too soon.

The one-point question: "What kind of investments are you looking for to get a maximum return for your $100,000?" gives you the opportunity to present the recommendation the reader expects you to make.

The second step in the selling-by-letter process should present interesting information about the features of the product or service. To create desire (D), slant the material, whenever possible, to the needs and wants of the customer. Discuss briefly only one or two features that might be of specific interest.

Unless requested, most readers of straight corporate sales letters do not want a "laundry list" at this stage.

The only readers who hang onto every word of a lengthy, information-packed, data-filled solicitation are those who enjoy advertisements concerned with their health or money. Don't expect such devotion to learning about other products.

The Big C is conviction. You are now ready to move into high gear, although a busy person may read only six to ten lines of this segment. Make them count. If you assume there are factors about which the reader may be in doubt, stress their values—but not for long. Don't belabor the points or the reader may feel too pressured. "Soft sell" has a better chance of enticing the reader toward conviction.

Here is where you put yourself more strongly in the prospect's place; anticipate possible objections and provide positive arguments—briefly. Suggest uses and advantages, and comment on the product's superiority because of design, utility and the like. Report the experience of users.

Now make your best and last move. Ask the reader to be a user. You ask for the business; you ask for action (A). If feasible, provide a tool: order blank, self-addressed card or offer a sample, a trial shipment, a meeting with a representative.

Although it may sound like a great deal to incorporate in one letter, the guidelines for any complete, correct and concise business communication will keep it short enough to be read attentively.

Unfortunately, most sales letters are too long, although they may be sparked by good facts in pleasing form. Mostly, it's the verbosity that turns the reader off.

For example: twelve simple words are more apt to be read and—understood: "Would your family have sufficient income should you be unable to work?" than these 38 words that carry less punch:

How do you see your insurance program in relation to your overall family security program to take care of their needs should you be unable to provide for them in the immediate future because of death and disability?

Often the card enclosed with the letter, intended to commit the customer to positive action, may be burdened by lengthy, unnecessary and sometimes demeaning instruction. For example: "In filling out this card, will you sign your name on the first line, and give your date of birth and place of business as well as country of origin?"

Most readers need only to be asked: "Would you please fill out all the information on this card?"

Every sales representative knows about negative verb questions—crafty devices that invariably lead the customer into an affirmative decision. They're used in the closing segment of most sales pitches and are no less effective in letter-writing. Example: "Isn't it better to install our equipment now, before your busy season begins?" provides a practical reason for a "Yes" reply. You will be ready, of course, to write up a follow-up letter that sets the schedule for installation and, later, send a bill. Which brings us to what to do after you make the sale. Collect.

Collection Letters

Always, the name of the game is to maintain a mutual association. It can be done even with collection letters.

Some do "come on strong." We know the weaknesses and strengths of various business writings, but the "strength" of the collection letter often becomes its "weakness."

Unlike St. Paul's "the spirit giveth life," it is the spirit (more aptly the attitude) of some collection letters that killeth the recipient's urge to pay.

Corporate dependence on the "dunning" system that requires a progressive psychological urging is becoming obsolete as business writing skills are updated and improved. One or two persuasive letters generally get results without the high cost of a long series of letters.

However, individual reaction remains unpredictable. This is why collection letters can often be more effective when they are dictated individually to deal with specific problems and types of delinquent accounts.

A letter to a retail customer would be written in a friendly, informal style. It might imply that nonpayment has been an oversight or it could appeal to the person's pride by mentioning that most credit customers pay their delinquent accounts when reminded. Hard pressure most always offends retail customers.

Wholesalers, as a rule, expect no more than the positive reminder that arrives 10 or 15 days after a nonpayment of an invoice. The language is brief, direct, but no less courteous and simply states the facts.

In either case, avoid generalities; they weaken the persuasion. One of the most common practices is to tell someone, however politely, that "payment should be within 30 days (or whatever) of the date of the letter." Carry the courtesy and the counting further: name the date, i.e., "by July 15." It's a convenience that will be appreciated.

Certainly, another collection letter would be unappreciated and, probably, useless, if you were to receive a reply like this: "I never ordered this Wonder Widget. If I did, you didn't send it. If you sent it, I never got it. If I got it, I paid for it. If I didn't, I won't."

Although this retort is more humorous than likely, it serves to show that Newton's law of physics: "To every action there is always an equal and opposite reaction" can be relevant to human behavior.

Resumés

We do know we are subject to the actions of others. Because of this many are toppled from high places, while others fall of their own weight. Thus, the need for resumés and application letters.

Not only the re-learning of good resumé writing may come in handy should you want to carve a new career, but it is most helpful in evaluating the job applications submitted for your consideration or final approval.

The planning of a resumé should include a list of facts and attributes which conform to the needs of a potential employer. In terms of the position sought, arrange these carefully. Work within a frame of categories: experience, education, personal and professional accomplishments, awards.

In effect, a resumé is a catalog of the positive and substantial contributions the applicant can make to an organization.

There are two methods of presentation. The first method lists jobs held, starting with the most recent. Also include titles and promotions, and the responsibilities within previous positions. When there is a strong continuity of work effort, this form is impressive when jobs are listed chronologically.

The second method emphasizes functions. Use specific illustrations from actual experiences to describe the function most closely related to the desired position. For example, one who applies for a position in your advertising department would add a more detailed job description to indicate familiarity with your corporate needs in this area.

COPYWRITER
XYZ Advertising Agency
(address)
Dec. 1, 1972–July 1, 1979

Assigned to writing annual reports, corporate and consumer literature, employee publications, sales presentations, radio and television commercials, direct-mail campaigns, print and outdoor advertising copy for 10 major corporate accounts. (List clients.)

Now prepare a formal data sheet headed with name, address, phone number(s) and Social Security number (for a touch of positive suggestion). List in order: Position Desired, Education, Experience and References. Such personal information as age and marital status rarely is required in view of today's anti-discrimination practices. (In time, both will be determined by other means.)

Application Letter

This catalog of expertise should be covered by an application letter. It is the ultimate sales letter because it intends to sell a valuable product—a human being's time and talents.

The tone of the letter that reflects the attitude of the applicant is most important. It also provides a clue to personality and character.

The use of *I* in an application letter does not violate the You Approach. *I,* in this case, stands for the product, provided its benefits to the reader are clearly stated.

The best attitude is neither timid, apologetic, boastful or overconfident—it is sincere. Nor should services be overvalued or undervalued; let the facts speak for themselves. A mention of the salary desired is usually withheld, unless it answers a specific request.

The ADCA formula of the sales letter is put to work with the opening sentence. Stereotyped introductions such as reference to an advertisement or "I am looking for a position . . ." are not good attention-getters.

Further, the more important qualifications should be stated in an unhackneyed way. "Fourteen years' experience on the management level of a Fortune 500 company, I believe, qualifies me to be your Executive Vice-President," says it all and simply.

Then, the desire for the applicant's services is created by emphasizing the contributions that will most benefit the company.

As you know, the final judgment of qualifications is the perrogative of the employer. An applicant should not write "I am well educated, ambitious, tactful, etc." The employer will draw the best conclusions from the hard facts in a well-prepared resumé and interesting letter.

Follow-up Letters

When you review applications, it is courteous to send acknowledgments and some indication that they are being considered. If, after a reasonable time, the applicant does not receive an acknowledgment, he or she should send a courteous and brief inquiry.

Even in the event of a negative response, the applicant should express appreciation for consideration. It may wield some influence at a later date.

Should an interview be granted, a letter of thanks is in order, no matter what the outcome.

Again, all these efforts portray an *attitude* that can influence the possibility of a lasting association. In this regard, the resumé, application letter and the follow-up have many of the same qualities as a sales pitch.

Letter of Inquiry and Form Letters

What is a letter of inquiry really expected to do? Know the answer precisely and you will begin the letter with a direct request.

Make your opening complete. If you are ordering literature, for instance, also identify the advertisement or any other source where you learned it was available. If you seek information out of the ordinary routine, as when you inquire about a prospective employee, the quality of a certain product and the like, be sure to add statements later that will support or explain your interest.

You may have to respond to inquiries by undisguised form letters. This seems acceptable, provided it acknowledges the inquiry pleasantly, says that the request is being complied with or the material is being sent, or tell where it may be demonstrated, inspected or obtained.

Form letters may be the only method that large companies have to cope with the demand for nationally advertised products, in particular. A small company, however, could benefit from individualized letters to potential customers instead of the typical form letter in stereotyped language devised for the sake of secretarial convenience. In this era of "intelligent" typewriters and other electronic communicators, whole phrases plucked from computer memories can assemble a "form" letter with more personal appeal.

An original answer to an inquiry is especially effective when the letter of inquiry provides a sales lead. The reply contains just enough information to sustain customer interest, with the main sales effort coming through a sales representative.

Order Letters

A western bookseller wrote to a firm in Chicago asking that a dozen copies of Canon Farrar's *Seekers After God* be shipped at once.

The publisher telegraphed this reply: "No seekers after God in Chicago or New York. Try Philadelphia."

As a general rule, only individuals and small business firms have occasion to write order letters. Purchase orders are more often used by large corporations.

Too many orders have been unfilled and misunderstood because of inaccurate listing. If a letter is to be written, you will be assured of accuracy when a rough memorandum of the material to be ordered is part of your planning.

Refer to the memorandum carefully and then give the information in this order: 1) quantity, 2) unit of measure, 3) catalog number, if available, 4) description or name of article, and 5) size, color, etc.

If required, mention the method of shipping desired in the opening paragraph that introduces the list.

When is acknowledgment of an order received usually required? It may not be necessary when the goods have been shipped promptly, accompanied by an invoice and you have good trade relations with a well-established vendor or customer.

Orders from new customers justify a prompt response as a matter of sales promotion. It's a good time to invite them to use other products or services—do a bit of "cross-selling."

Claim and Adjustment Letters

A small plaque on the desk of the president of a major corporation reads: "DEBSWPALP!" It stands for an important rule in business: "Don't Ever Be Surprised When People Act Like People."

This is why there are times when both seller and buyer must make concessions—the seller, if the complaint of the customer is justified; the buyer, if the complaint is unfounded. And so, we need special letters for special people.

All customer complaints should find their way to a tactful letter-writer who has a cooperative attitude. Then the reply is more apt not only to maintain good will, but, in spite of adverse conditions, to guide its return to your company.

The most common complaints arise from errors made in handling large, active accounts. Although the errors be irritating, angry language only magnifies the error. (Remember, a learned man errs with a learned error; when an entry is placed in the debit column instead of in the credit column, it may be only because the clerk is left-handed!)

The adjustment that does not satisfy a customer's claim can be a costly victory in terms of losing future business and good will. A forward-looking attitude should influence such a letter, so that the aggrieved customer will feel reconciled and remain a profitable outlet for your company's products or services.

A reluctant or grudging attitude is fatal to the good-will possibilities. Would you like to receive a letter that begins: "At your insistence and in spite of the fact that investigation shows that we are not at fault, we are granting the adjustment claimed in your letter dated August 1."

It's an attitude of corporate confidence that counts: "The fairness you have shown in all our dealings prompts us to grant, without further inquiry, the adjustment. . . ." Or simply grant the request with friendly finality like this: "Our dealers certainly should not be penalized for an occasional error. We are glad, therefore, to accept the unsold merchandise as you suggested."

Almost any letter-writer can accede gracefully; to refuse a claim requires tact of a higher order. There is nothing more difficult than the art of making a refusal agreeable.

In this case, it's positioning that makes it artful. The plan and structure of such a letter is a reversal of the usual order in which you state your purpose clearly at the outset. The refusal comes late instead of early.

In most cases, placating the claimant would be more difficult in the beginning because the explanation would come as a sort of anticlimax. It's a reasonable assumption that this vital phase of the letter will be read more attentively and soften the blow if it comes before rather than after the refusal.

There is one exception: when you know one of your clients would prefer to "know the worst" early and would regard the delay as beating about the bush. Then, state the denial in regretful tones immediately.

Normally, the preferred topical sequence is: 1) a sympathetic, friendly approach, 2) a tactful review of the situation, 3) a courteous denial, 4) an optimistic closing that looks forward to future association, etc.

Credit Letters

A letter refusing credit also calls for a slight delay in mentioning the bad news. When you do, soften it by a kind of courteous hedging that also means what it says: "The situation at this time does not warrant a charge account."

Be sure to follow this with a short paragraph or two expressing gratitude for the interest and confidence shown by the applicant and an invitation to use the facilities or products on a cash basis.

Granting credit by letter is a more pleasurable exercise. You will display your enthusiasm and review the benefits of having established credit with your company.

Letter to Congress

"Today, there were four letters about the high cost of postal service—all from the same person!" The inconsistency of purpose seemed to bewilder the Congressional aide who confided the problems of screening about 4,000 letters a week.

It also inspired some advice about letters to Capitol Hill. We all know that members of Congress like to keep in touch with constituents, especially those responsible for employment. Send along the annual reports and occasional courtesy letters mentioning awards or benefits to employees, a new corporate policy, invention or product that will improve the area's economic climate or any phase of your operation that is of special interest to the legislator.

Then, when a more serious issue arises, the contact already has been maintained or initiated. For instance, if you want to complain about a proposed bill that may be harmful to your company's interest or any other serious matter, this letter has a better chance of getting a personal reading because of previous and agreeable communication.

When the problem is of broader concern and needs the attention of a group of key legislators or a regulatory agency, check the committee assignments that should be kept updated in the files of your legal or public affairs department. Match your communication purpose to the proper person; re-routing in Washington is a risk.

Remember, members of Congress usually don't open their own mail. They depend on trained staffers to weed out offensive messages from cranks. Form letters have virtually no impact. The exceptions, today, may have been disguised by computerization. It is always better to produce individualized letters that can carry a line or two that directly relates to each legislator's special interest (although the same basic message is sent to several members of a committee).

There's a best way to get the attention you deserve: write a good letter! They seem to be so rare, yours will command attention.

Make your point clearly and concisely, anticipate the questions (and some answers), and establish a connection between your concern or problem and the state or district in which the legislator is especially concerned. Don't forget to write a thank-you letter for any services or information.

If possible, time your letter to avoid the heavier mail deliveries on Mondays and Fridays. Besides, those days are travel times for many who commute to and from their districts. It's better to mail your letter(s) to arrive at midweek.

Before you seal the envelope, check two vital factors. First, the information: did you drown the issue in a flood of facts and statistics? Second, check its tone: does it reflect a cooperative attitude? Did you compose it in any kind of emotional state, even if you feel wronged? Our legislators, like other executives, are too busy to plow through outrageous, grandiose statements. Your letter may never get past the Congressional aide.

Ultimately, as you do in all writing, you may again consider the old Chinese proverb: "In the midst of a great joy, do not promise to give a (wo)man anything; in the midst of great anger, do not answer a letter."

Economy has frequently nothing to do with the amount being spent but with the wisdom used in spending it.
— Henry Ford

10.

The Bottom Line

Cost and Effect of Communication

Wordy documents are overrunning the business world. When they are not useful or effective, there is waste. Waste, whatever its source, dramatically affects the corporate balance sheet.

To arrive at where we are going, we must know where to begin. And we begin by being more realistic about the estimated cost of $5.59 (1979 study: Dartnell Institute of Business Research) to get one business letter from your head to another person's desk. (In 1953, the cost was $1.17; in 1938, 50 cents!)

Today, if you have only 50 people in your company each writing five letters a day, five days a week, it costs your company $363,350 a year. This year.

Salaries double, productivity doesn't. People working with pencils and typewriters can't produce any more for $12,000 a year than they can for $6,000. Secretaries using standard machines are still producing usable words in the same length of time they did ten years ago.

If you're still dictating a few years from now, a heavier workload (due to business growth) may slow you up. Further, the increase in the value of your executive time is sure to contribute to the higher cost of written communication.

As your correspondence and in-house communiques increase in volume, further delegation of writing chores may not be a practical or possible solution nor will it substantially lower the cost when you have to hire writing specialists to do the job—or do it yourself.

Even today, the demand simply outweighs the supply of willing workers with extraordinary writing skills and an updated knowledge of good business English.

We are beginning to understand that the qualities that make an outstanding executive secretary and administrative assistant are also among the qualities needed on higher rungs of the corporate ladder.

While many office workers are moving up, others are moving away from routine clerical and secretarial functions into more exciting fields that offer greater career opportunities and higher pay. Further, the age of computerization has brought us programmers, typographers, electronic word processor operators, etc., and with it, their proficiency in the use of language.

Computerization, in itself, may be largely responsible for the new executive focus of interest on the quality, quantity and cost of corporate communications. Words are big business.

Cutting the Costs—and Your Habits

Let's look at the national level: Americans mail at least 54 billion business messages a year. Of that number, let us assume one-third represents personally dictated messages. At a minimum cost of six dollars each, (including expenses for personnel, material, processing and postage), the one-third of 54 billion (or 18 billion) messages costs at least 108 *billion* dollars in a fiscal year.

If we improve business correspondence so that the cost is cut by a mere 10 percent, at least 10 billion dollars can be saved annually. This enormous sum could then be used to improve operations, products and services, thereby benefitting business and industry, its employees, the public and the economy.

Improvement begins with you. Labor cost is the heart of the cost problem in business writing. No executive needs to be reminded that "Time is money," as Ben Franklin said. Thus when your habits really save time, you get lower unit writing costs. For instance, is your method of working really right for you?

Is your time being put to its best use? Would your letters be more effective if they were dictated early in the morning rather than later? Would you have less need to make time-consuming changes if you drafted carefully thought out texts or outlines in longhand on legal pads? If you hand-write messages and instructions, are they hard-to-read? (A study, conducted by *Modern Office Procedures* magazine and a trade organization, says that 79 percent of the businesses surveyed report losses due to bad handwriting.)

Do you come to the writing job "cold," or do you jot down and file ideas, phrases, suggestions for future correspondence; plot strategies and note them; think through each message before writing or dictating?

Is each message's effectiveness your prime concern, regardless of its author? Messages for which you are responsible, if only by your signature, are considered profitable by the quality of their effectiveness. The cost/effect ratio is the final judge. Nothing else is.

Sales loss is an obvious cost. It happens when a customer is not contacted, not persuaded, not brought to the point of action or not reassured. The right kind of explanation and appeals can increase production or make a sales effort rewarding.

The greatest cost of written communication is in the actual writing. Can you now turn out complete, concise, correct and coherent letters, memos and the rest? Are other writers in your company appropriately employed? If you delegate your writing chores, does your alter ego have modern business writing expertise? Does your department or company have a writing style manual to be used as reference? If so, is it geared to an economy of words? Check these out first, then turn to typing, transcription, reproduction, paper and paper costs.

Paper Costs Count

Even after the J. C. Penney Company was doing a volume of business of hundreds of thousands of dollars, overhead expenses were kept down so that the price of merchandise could remain low. When mail came in, Mr. Penney personally slit the envelopes and used the blank sides for scratch paper. In time, such austerity was considered unnecessary.

Minnesota Mining & Manufacturing Company uses 10 million sheets of stationery a year, according to

Henry Owen, a 3M executive. And that's typical of the paper blizzard inundating many large corporations!

Robert Metz, in his book *CBS: Reflections in a Bloodshot Eye,* tells how that corporation had 78 different letterheads, five different kinds of paper and three different sizes of stationery. Frank Stanton, then Columbia Broadcasting System's president, and Lou Dorfsman, design head, standardized the paper for a $150,000-a-year saving. Stanton also established a specific format for secretaries and others to follow in observing margins and spacing paragraphs.

Further, many companies are cutting back on the size of annual reports because of rising paper and production costs. A *Wall Street Journal Business Bulletin* (1/24/80) says Equimark will use 16 fewer pages and fewer photos in its 1980 report, while Itel Corporation slashed its report to 40 pages from 68 and abandoned glossy paper. Petrolite Corporation eliminates color photos and adds a "paper bag" cover. "We don't want to appear ostentatious," an executive says.

All of this is often given priority during cutback binges, but rarely is equal time given to the cost/effect ratio of the actual business writing. Matching its quality to the quality of a prestigious logo and expensive rag bond or improving its effect to enhance less impressive stationery is also efficient.

Automatic Typewriters and Word Processors

Turning to resources which can be controlled to increase profits indicates a shift in perception from office cost-cutting to an emphasis on increasing management and organizational productivity.

The most commonly used and less costly resource is the automatic typewriter that allows the operator to make changes in a first-typed version, then lets the machine do the final re-typing and produce hordes of duplicates.

For years, the investment in secretaries, typists and professionals who do a lot of writing has been relatively low. But, as labor costs rose and the labor force grew, the need to improve productivity became more pressing.

Fortunately, technological advances have made the equipment more economical to use. Nevertheless, while the cost of computer innards continues to decline, the costs of software and support services seem to be rising.

Wherever increased productivity is essential to the profit structure, the heavier cost ot technological aids is justified. Productivity may increase as much as 40 percent with the help of "intelligent typewriters" and other devices with computer memories. Also, management time is saved by reducing proofreading to the changes made to a revised document.

The quality depends on the input and the choice of stored material. There's little excuse for delaying the task of writing letters, memos, reports and proposals when there is a judicious retrieval of stored information.

The new automation brings the user into a stronger position to exercise choice. Moving information electronically takes little personal effort and energy, but it does increase the need for good original thinking, diction, composition and qualified judgment.

The word-processing operation is now considered a profession. Seventy-five operators who attended the first seminar sponsored by Word Processing Society, Inc. helped to make it so. They decided "Word-Processing Specialist" should be the title used to identify their profession. While "typist," "operator" and "secretary" may be good or appropriate, those names really no longer apply.

Although machines are proficient in the generation, handling, storage, retrieval, communication and utilization of information, human brains put thoughts and ideas into useable words. "Garbage in, garbage out" is as viable a statement today as it was when the computers first made the scene.

Short is always better, but not always best. Let's not get caught up in the wake of increased productivity so that we lose the niceties in a computer.

For instance, keyboarders, in particular, tend to abbreviate names, places and title. Insist that names be written out; abbreviations give an impression of hasty unconcern. Certainly it's proper to abbreviate states, but not preferable. And if you're interested in good will, don't abbreviate a person's title or tamper with a name. Names are precious; hand a person a pen to try and see what he or she writes with it!

For the same reason, form letters with the name obviously filled in with a different type style or inserted out-of-line by an inexpert typist are often offensive. Happily, personalization by computer has almost convinced readers that they have a name and not a number.

The Selectric typewriter with a magnetic-tape memory used mostly for form letters was the first word processor. It was introduced by IBM in 1964. This was followed in the mid-seventies by word processors offering, among other marvels, video display on a cathode-ray tube. It was only a beginning; the waves of technological change roll on. There's a wide variety of peripheral devices such as graphic and high-speed line printers to match almost any application you need. An ordinary telephone line can transmit volumes of data in a minute through an electronic switching system.

The new market potential for "talking" typewriters linked to each other, embraces 13 million business offices. If only two percent of these offices become in-office typographic centers, yours may be one of the 260,000.

Stand-alone word processors with video displays flashing documents long distance from one processor to another are the fastest growing segment of the word-processing market. Shipments are expected to increase at an annual rate of 50 percent, compounded, through 1984.

Large corporations opt for several units hooked together, sharing the memory of a central computer.

Data Corporation, an independent research firm, estimates the market for word processors might reach $4.2 billion in the U.S. by 1984.

Profits, not prophets, foretell the future. Will these modern masters of communication be practical aids to your profit structure?

Add the cost of word processing to the price tags of telecommunication systems and increased labor costs and the "bottom line" takes a beating—unless the increased production of effective messages and the prudent use of easily obtained and accurate information justifies the cost.

Never was clarity and conciseness more important. The challenge is yours to provide proper input for the electronic output. Words are still master! There is no longer an excuse for making a letter longer because you lack the time to make it shorter.

Less paperwork, less waste. Less corrections; less paperwork. The Commission on Federal Paperwork once used 1,605 sheets of paper to ask members of Congress for their help in cutting down on unnecessary paperwork. The second letter followed the first because two lines of printing instructions had been included accidentally in the first. They also got another letter apologizing for the first letter. Don't let it happen to you!

Electronic Mail Delivery

Now there is another threat to bloat mailing costs. The huge deficit-prone U.S. Postal Service is expected to be revitalized largely by additional hikes in postal rates. Congressional authorities gravely warn: "Unless the Postal Service is thoroughly overhauled, rates could rise as high as one dollar for first class mail in a matter of years."

The General Accounting office already predicts the cost of mailing a letter could go up to 34 cents if the service is to break even by 1984. All the more reason to make each letter do the job for which it is intended!

Further, outgoing Postmaster General Benjamin F. Bailar, during his final appearance on Capitol Hill in March, 1978, said daily mail delivery probably will not be financially feasible by the year 2000.

Of course, rising costs will be passed on to users, not taxpayers. The biggest users are businesses. But greater satisfaction, at least, may be on the way. Automation is expected to make the whole system more efficient and productive, if not less costly.

For instance, the Postal Service is taking a close look at two systems now in the test mode: Intelpost and ECOM.

International Electronic Post uses high speed digital fax to scan letters and send them via satellite to receiving post offices in other countries. It functions as a type of high-speed electronic copier service, enabling users to send exact copies of messages, drawings, medical records, engineering plans, etc., between the United States and selected countries.

Sylvia Porter, renowned business columnist, tells us the transmission cost of this service is projected at less than five dollars per 8½-by-11 or 14-inch size page. Transmission time to London, as an illustration, is three minutes.

ECOM (for electronic computer-originated mail) would use Western Union as the carrier. This system is similar to mailgram except that input is electronic instead of by paper or dictation.

As of early 1980, these services await approval by the Federal Communications Commission.

Mailing Efficiency

Being aware of the inadequacy of certain operational methods you have been taking for granted may also stimulate cost-cutting measures and certainly cut back the production of *useless* mail. An analysis of the mail "flow" leaving your office would be helpful.

What is the average out-going mail volume per week? Is the "flow" steady or are there monthly and seasonal variations? What percentage of the mail is sent "first class?" Could some letters be mailed at a cheaper rate such as second, third or fourth class? How many letters do you personally receive each day? How many answers can you comfortably produce? What is the overall mail-load for your company? (The DuPont Company mailroom handles six tons of mail daily.) Is it sorted and distributed efficiently without delay or error?

A new insight may lead you to seek professional advice on reducing mailing costs. Consult with a local post office official or write to Postal Education Center, Pitney Bowes, Pacific and Walnut Streets, Stamford, Connecticut 06904.

Here are a few money-saving tips: When you need only a receipt to prove delivery, switch to certified mail from the registered mail that is costing approximately three times more. Cost of overseas correspondence can be cut considerably by using aerogrammes that include stationery and stamp. When time is money, consider express mail that guarantees delivery of an item from your post office to the addressee's post office in 24 hours. For a cost of one-third or less, priority mail delivers packages anywhere in the United States directly to the addressee within one to three days. It also provides options such as insurance, COD, return receipts and restricted delivery.

Mailgrams, sent electronically to any local post office in the United States, are delivered with the next business day's mail.

Also, check out the low cost of parcel airlift mail (PAL) when sending parcels to military personnel abroad.

The availability of new methods of message delivery compels us, as never before, to consider more carefully the effect/cost ratio measure of our own business writing and the efforts of others.

Summing It Up

To determine the effects and thus the real costs, probe for *facts* and *feedback* by asking yourself and others: 1) What can we dispense with? 2) What writing or dictating skills need fundamental improvement? 3) What do we really know about the efficiency of the various forms and the impact of form letters upon readers?

Move on to study the production of business messages with special attention to the procedures and the expertise of office staff and writers. If you find an immediate economy, be sure it is not at the expense of another aspect of business writing.

Research is a costly item in terms of time and talent. Is it actually put to work through proposals and reports? The cost of research time should be spread over a number of applications, wherever feasible.

John D. Rockefeller, Sr. once said: "The ability to deal with people is as purchasable a commodity as sugar or coffee. And I will pay more for that ability than for any other under the sun." Letters that foster good customer relations prove the value of your ability. Your readers are likely to say, "Here is a person with whom I'd like to do business." That's the executive commodity that leads to profit.

Check the accuracy of information. Many an order has been botched, requests ignored, explanations misunderstood and sales lost because of incomplete, incorrect and careless communication.

The rising cost of paper products should foster a search for reliable substitutes. Re-evaluate the quality and quantity, as well as the initial cost, of the stationery, business cards, forms, pre-printed materials etc.

In all these areas—and wherever you search for the true effect/cost of written communication—aim to deliver the best possible impact with the least possible input.

For this, join with the efficiency experts when they look at the whole corporate picture and find an important part of the rising cost problem is ineffective communication.

Not even the experts will advocate reaching impatiently for shortcuts to efficient business writing. On that route, the stuff from which profits really are made—clarity and force—is often lost. The only shortcut to improving business is to know the pitfalls and avoid them gracefully.

As you plan to trailblaze through foggy writing and the paper blizzard, cutting costs along the way, you may need the impetus of this advice from the late John Henry Newman: "Nothing would be done at all if persons waited until they could do it so well that no one could find fault with it."

Decalogue
Lights To Write By

I. Think first, for only fools record their bombast and blunders in writing.

II. Employ a conversational style, provided the language is neither ambiguous, sensual nor profane.

III. Strive for brevity and simplicity, as time to say what must be said is fleeting.

IV. Avoid grammatical liberties, for they offend those who know better and confuse those who do not.

V. Avoid gruffness, circumvention and pomposity. They smudge the company image and your own.

VI. Be not distracted, disturbed, diffident or dilatory during dictation.

VII. Begin by saying what you propose to say, then say it, and close by saying succinctly what you have said.

VIII. Abhor outmoded phrases, jargon, sexist language and sesquipedality.

IX. Regard each reader as a friend, for one who departs from this edict soon may be friendless.

X. Call upon others to produce useful and effective written communication in the name of the corporate gods of cost and customer relations.

Epilogue
The Paperless World Beyond

As this book goes to press, the attention of corporate America is focused on top executives who are pulling the plugs on their costly, but baffling computer terminals.

It seems that paperless technology, for all its benefits, may have its limitations. Are we really ready for the ultimate in sophisticated communication? What of the many managers who are still groping for the ways and means to communicate clearly, concisely, and completely on paper? Now they are expected to push all the right keys on a computer terminal with the unhesitating finesse of a veteran professional business writer. Their messages are no longer tucked in envelopes and file folders but flashed on television-like screens at the flick of a button.

According to Lawrence Rout's page one *Wall Street Journal* article (June 24, 1980), ". . . professionals and executives are being forced to make major psychological and behavioral adjustments as they move into a paperless world. They must get used to, among other things, infallible computers that remind bosses when reports are due, the pressure of always being reachable through a portable computer terminal, and the danger of overcommunication."

All this is true, but let's look at a basic, unmentioned problem: Pressured by communication experts who believe it crucial that this new way of business be fully accepted, few executives will admit that the old way still needs improvement. Yet, everyone should understand that until the techniques of business writing are thoroughly absorbed and practiced, computerization, with all its advantages, cannot appreciably improve the *quality* of communication. Without this improvement, it is as ineffective as ever.

Certainly, it increases the *quantity*. While you are making an effort to reduce a two-page letter to one page, others are using costly computer time and equipment to transmit their usual excessive verbiage within and outside corporate walls. Wherever overcommunication was a problem, it is likely to be compounded by those who bring their long-practiced disregard for conciseness to terminal keyboards.

As the *WSJ* reports, "Many top managers resist paperless technology for their own offices and for many reasons." Nevertheless, the important reasons cited do not include the discomfort of many executives when they tangle with the written word under any circumstances.

A lack of technical knowledge of computer operation may not be the only basis for "looking like a jerk." Some may simply be fearful that a barrage of bombast and blunders previously committed to paper will be far more evident when the message is on the screen for everyone to see.

It seems far better to attribute their resistance to other reasons. Change, for instance. Executives, in particular, find it time-consuming and, sometimes, unnecessary to forego time-worn but usually successful systems.

John Connell, executive director of the Office of Technology Research Group, Pasadena, California, as quoted in *WSJ* recognizes the behavioral problem. "Everytime we design a system," he says, "we do it on the premise that the people must adapt to the system. I think we have to adopt an ethic that says we adapt machinery to people."

Today, those who would rather talk than write are expected to trade dictation time for a session pecking at a keyboard. (Many can't type anyway.) Meetings, although preferred by many, are being replaced by electronically transmitted information, ideas, and discussions, in the interest of time management.

There are also many executives who find it difficult to accept the totally impersonal flavor of computerized customer and employee communications. A well-written letter or memo, worked and re-worked on paper has always met special needs. Only when a keyboard can be manipulated with equally effective results, will there be a smooth and satisfying move into the paperless business world.

Further, because of the excitement generated by a new automated tool, management can easily be inundated with worthless information. Now, more than ever, lengthy, padded reports and proposals will be written to impress rather than express. The cost escalates with the need for computerized storage and retrieval of largely valueless material. Simplified language, fed into memory banks, can turn the situation around. Well-written and needed information, conveyed quickly by automation, substantially increases productivity. And that's the name of the game.

For this purpose, and in spite of current resistance by those whose terminals now face the wall, paperless technology is here to stay.

We have only to remember that words come first and learn to use them with greater wisdom and economy.

Reams of paper may be replaced by visual aids, but communication begins in the human brain for which there will be no substitute.

Frances D. Naczi

Bibliography

Recommended Reading

Bromage, Mary C. *Writing Audit Reports.* New York: John Wiley and Sons, 1974.

Cottam, Keith M. & Pelton, Robert W. *Writer's Research Handbook.* New York: Barnes & Noble, 1978.

Ewing, David W. *Writing for Results in Business, Government & the Professions.* 2nd ed. New York: McGraw-Hill, 1979.

Flesch, Rudolf. *The Art of Readable Writing.* 25th ed. New York: Harper & Row, 1974.

Flesch, Rudolf. *The Art of Plain Talk.* New York: Collier Books, 1974.

Gunning, Robert. *Techniques of Clear Writing.* New York: rev. ed. McGraw-Hill, 1968.

Hayakawa, S.I., et al. *Language in Thought & Action.* 4th ed. New York: Harcourt Brace Jovanovich, 1972.

Hayakawa, S.I. *The Use & Misuse of Language.* New York: Fawcett, 1975.

Kett, Merriellyn & Underwood, Virginia. *How to Avoid Sexism: A Guide for Writers, Editors & Publishers.* Chicago: Laurence Ragan Communication, Inc., 1978.

Kredenser, Gail. *Write It Right.* New York: Barnes & Noble, 1972.

Lewis, Phillip & Baker, William H. *Business Report Writing.* Columbus, Ohio: Grid Publishers, Inc., 1978.

McCrimmon, James M. *Writing With a Purpose.* 6th ed. Mass: Houghton Mifflin Co., 1975.

Menzel, Donald H., et al. *Writing a Technical Paper.* New York: McGraw-Hill, 1972.

Michaels, Leonard and Ricks, Christopher. *The State of the Language.* Berkeley, CA., University of California Hess, 1979.

Newman, Edwin. *Strictly Speaking.* New York: Warner Books, 1975.

Payne, Lucille V. *The Lively Art of Writing.* New York: New American Library, 1969.

Shaw, Harry. *Writing & Rewriting.* 5th ed. New York: Harper & Row, 1973.

Smith, Randi S. *Written Communication for Data Processing.* Van Nostrand Reinhold, 1976.

University of Chicago. *A Manual of Style.* Chicago: University of Chicago Press, 1969.

Dictionaries

Webster's Third New International Dictionary of the English Language. Springfield, Mass.: G. & C. Merriam Co., 1964.

Funk & Wagnalls New Standard Desk Dictionary. New York: T.Y. Crowell, 1977.

The American Heritage Dictionary of the English Language. Boston: Houghton Mifflin Co. 1969.

Random House Unabridged Dictionary of the English Language. Stein, J. and Urdang L., eds. New York: Random House, 1966.

The Oxford English Dictionary. England: Clarendon Press, 1933. (13 vols.)

Subject Dictionaries

Acronyms, Initialisms & Abbreviations Dictionary. Detroit, Mich.: Gale Research Co., 1978--1980.

Black's Law Dictionary. St. Paul, Minn.: West Publishing Co.

Cowan, Henry J. *Dictionary of Architectural Science.* New York: Halsted Press, Div. of John Wiley, 1973.

Good, Carter V., ed. *Dictionary of Education.* New York: McGraw-Hill, 1973.

Hayakawa, S.I., ed. *Funk & Wagnalls Modern Guide to Synonyms and Related Words.* New York: Funk & Wagnalls, 1968.

Kohler, Eric L. *Dictionary for Accountants.* 5th ed. New Jersey: Prentice-Hall, 1975.

Kent, Ruth K. *The Language of Journalism: A Glossary of Print-Communications Terms.* Ohio: Kent State Univ. Press, 1970.

McGraw-Hill Dictionary of Modern Economics: a Handbook of Terms and Organizations. 2nd ed. New York: McGraw-Hill, 1973.

McGraw-Hill Dictionary of Scientific and Technical Terms. New York: McGraw-Hill, 1974.

INDEX

ADCA, 134-137, 141
Absolute phrase, 68
Action
    closings of letters and, 45, 46
    sales letters and, 136-137
Active verbs, 56-58
Adjectives, use with, verbs, 57-58
Adjustment letters, 144-146
Adverb
    clauses, 78
    conjunctive, 70
    position of, 73
    split infinitive and, 63-64
Aerogrammes, 159
Agenda preparation, 119
Annual reports, paper costs of, 153
Anti-discrimination, *see* Sexist language
Apologetic opening, of a letter, 41-42
Application letter, 140-141
    follow-up letter to, 141-142
Articles, sexist language and, 91
Associated Press Style Book, The, 64
Attention, sales letters and, 135
Attitude, of letters, 133
    see also Letters, types of
Automatic typewriters, 153-154
Automation
    electronic mail delivery, 157-158
    typewriters, 153-154

Beginning of a letter, *see* letter, opening of
Bureaucracy, *see* Government
Burke, Edmund, 11
Business writing
    amount of, 151
    awareness of need for effective, 16
    concept of, 23
    purpose of, 20-21, 75
    reasons for mistakes in, 7-8
    responsibility for, 16-17
    timing, 23-24
    see also Simplification; specific types (i.e. Letter; Report, etc.)
Business writing, costs of, 149-150, 160-161

automatic typewriters, 153-154
electronic mail delivery, 157-158
mailing efficiency, 9, 158-159
morale and efficiency, 11-12
savings in, 151-152
support staffs, 9-10
paper, 9, 152-153, 160-161
word processors, 154-157

CBS: Reflections in a Bloodshot Eye, 153
Califano, Joseph A., 10
Capitalization, 167
Carter, President Jimmy salutations and, 33
Catchall words, 26
Certified mail, 159
"Chair," use of, 94-95
Chief Executives' Handbook, 92
Churchill, Sir Winston, 63, 71-72
Claim letters, 144-146
Clauses
    adverb, 78
    in sentence construction, 66-67
    semicolons used with, 69
    "that" and "which" and, 58-59
Clichés, 26
Closing of a letter, *see* Letter, closing of
Collection letters, 44-45, 81, 137-139
Colloquialisms, 65-66
Comma, 67-69, 73
Complaints, adjustment letters and, 144-146
Complex phrases, 77
Compliments, in opening of letter, 43
Compound sentences, 69, 74
Computers
    costs and, 154
    form letters and, 14-15
    word processing and, 154-157
    see also Automation
Conclusion, of a letter, *see* Letters, closing of
Confirmation, You Approach and, 39

Congress, letters to, 146-148
Conjunctions, 61-62
Conjunctive adverb, 70
Contractions, 64-65
Contract, proposals and, 129-132
Conviction, sales letters and, 136
Costs, *see* Business writing, costs of
Credit letters, 146
Customer complaints, adjustment letters and, 144-146

Dartnell Institute of Business Research, 9, 149-150
Delegation, dictation and, 107-108
Delivery, of letter, 24-25
Desire, sales letters and, 135-136
Dictation, 13-14, 99-100
    of the Amiable, 106-107
    of collection letters, 138
    costs of, 151
    of the Delegators, 107-108
    of the Erratic, 101
    guidelines for, 108-110
    of the Hedger, 104-106
    of the Mumbler, 103-104
    of the Orator, 102
    planning a letter and, 21
    of the Rambler, 100-101
    of the Rapid Fire Dictator, 103
Discrimination, *see* Sexist language

Education, word usage and, 55
Effect/cost ratios, *see* Business writing, costs of
Efficiency, poor communication and, 11-12
Electronic computer-originated mail (ECOM), 158
Eliot, George, 102
Emerson, Ralph Waldo, 134
Empathy, 39, 41-42
Ending, of a letter, *see* Letters, closing of
Equality, *see* Sexist language
Erratic speech, dictation and, 101
Evaluation, Memo as, 116
Express mail, 159

Feminist movement, *see* Sexist language
Filing, opening sentences and, 37
First person, *see* "I"

Flattery, in opening of letter, 43
Follow-up letters, 141-142
    application letter, 140-141
Ford, President Gerald R., 81-82
Foreword, for formal report, 123
Formal report, 123-127
Form letters, 14-15, 142-143
Forms
    as memos, 117-118
    progress reports and, 121-123

"Gentlemen," use of, 95
Glover, John D., 92
"Golden Shovel," 10
Good will
    in closing of a letter, 46
    dictation and, 106-107
    You Approach and, 39
Government
    paperwork and, 157
    sexist language and, 84, 93, 96
    simplification in language of, 10
Grammar, 56
    adjectives, 57-58
    capitalization, 67
    colloquialisms, 65-66
    conjunctions, 61-62
    contractions, 64-65
    importance of, 12
    nouns, 59-60
    paragraph placement, 67
    phrase elimination, 60-61
    prepositions, 62-63
    punctuation, 67-70
    sentence construction, 66-67
    sexist language and, 91-93
    split infinitives, 63-64
    "that" properly used, 58-59
    underlining, 67
    verbs, 56-58
    "which" properly used, 58-59

Handwriting, costs of bad, 151
"Headline salutation," 34
Hedging, dictation and, 104-106
House organ, 119
Humor, in opening of letter, 42

Ideas, expressing, 71-72
    avoiding misunderstanding 72-74
    paragraph cohesion, 79-82

purpose defined, 75
reinforcing, 76-78
simple sentences, 74
topic sentence, 76-78
Illustrations
of a formal report, 124
of a proposal, 131
Infinitives, split, 63-64
Informal Business Report, 120-121
Information, memo and, 114-115
Inquiry, letter of, 142-143
Instruction, memo as, 115
"International Electronic Post
(Intelpost)," 158
Introduction, of formal report, 124
see also Letters, opening of
"I," use of, 39-40
in application letter, 141
in dictation, 105
in formal business reports,
120-121

Job stereotypes, 86-88
see also Sexist language
Job titles, sexist language and,
96-97

Kitchelt, William H., 55

Language, de-sexing, *see* Sexist
language
Legislators, letters to, 146-148
Letters, closing of, 15-16, 45-48
salutation, 34
"Sincerely" used in, 47
You Approach in, 46
Letters, opening of, 15-16, 21,
31-32
apologetic, 41-42
answering a proposal, 36-37
being different, 40-41
filing purposes and, 37
flattery in, 43
humor in, 42
importance of, 32-33
persuasion in, 43-45
phrases in, 60
pronouns, 39-40
purpose defined in, 75
salutation, 33-34
setting the tone, 35-37
topic sentences, 35-38, 76-78
You Approach, 37-39
Letters, types of, 14-15, 133

application, 140-141
claim and adjustment,
144-146
collection, 44-45, 81, 137-139
to Congress, 146-148
credit, 146
follow-up, 141-142
form, 142-143
of inquiry, 142-143
memo and, 112, 118
order, 143-144
resume, 139-140
sales, 46, 66-67, 133-137
transmittal, 123
see also Business writing

"McGraw-Hill Book Company,
Guidlines for Equal Treatment
of the Sexes," 85-88
Mail
costs of, 9, 157-158
efficiency of, 158-159
use of, 24-25
Mailgram, 158, 159
Mailroom procedures, 159
Males, sexist language and, 93-94
see also Sexist language
Manuals, 118
Media, corporate communication
and, 119
Meetings
agenda for, 119
memos used instead of,
113-114
Memos, 111
compared with letter, 112, 118
language of, 113-114
manuals, 118
media, 119
newsletters, 119
meeting agenda, 119
necessity of, 116-117
pre-printed, 117-118
reasons for, 114-116
when to write, 111-112, 113-
114
Men, avoiding discrimination and,
86
see also Sexist language
"Miss," use of, 95-96
Misunderstanding, avoiding,
72-74
Morale
memo used for, 115

poor communication and,
11-12
"Mr.," use of, 95-96
"Mrs.," use of, 95-96
"Ms.," use of, 95-96
Mumbling, dictation and, 103-104

Negatives, avoiding, 81
Newman, John Henry, 161
Newsletters, 119
Nominalization, 59
Non-sexist language, see
Sexist language
Nouns, 59-60

Occupations, titles of, 96-97
Openings, of a letter, see Letters
opening of
Opposition, recommendation
reports and, 128
Order letters, 143-144
Outline
of formal report, 123
of proposal, 130

Paper, costs of, 9, 152-153, 160-161
Paragraph
cohesion among, 79-82
placement of, 67
topic sentence of, 78
Parcel Airlift Mail (PAL), 159
Paranthetical clauses, 58-59, 66-67
Parenthetical phrases, 68
Participial phrase, 68
Passive verb, 56-58, 105
Period, 68
"Person," avoiding sexism and,
94-95
Persuasion
collection letters as, 137-139
memo as, 115-116
in opening of a letter, 43-45
Phrases
commas used with, 68
complex, 77
elimination of, 60-61
misplaced, 73
parenthetical, 68
participial, 68
Planning, 15, 19-21, 29
beginning, 21
delivery of letter, 24-25
locating information, 23
purpose, 20-21
reason for writing, 24

timing, 23-24
what must be written, 22-23
who receives letter, 21-22
Pope, Alexander, 29
Porter, Sylvia, 158
Postage, costs of, 9
see also Mail
Postal service, see Mail
Prepositions, 62-63
Pre-printed forms
as memos, 117-118
as progress reports, 121-123
Presiding officer, form of address,
94-95
Priority mail, 159
Progress reports, 121-123
Pronouns
paragraph cohesion and, 79
sexist language and, 91-92
use of, 39-49
Proposal, 129-132
answering a, 36-37
Publishing, sexist language and,
85-88
Punctuation, 67-70
comma, 67-69, 73
idea expression and, 73
period, 68
semicolon, 67-70
Purpose, of a letter, 20-21, 75

Rambling, dictation and, 100-101
Reader's Digest, sentence length
of, 51
Recipient of letter, planning for
21-22
Recommendation reports, 128-129
Redundancy, 51, 52, 60
formal reports and, 126
reinforcing ideas by, 77
Registered mail, 159
Reminder, memo as, 114
Repetition
paragraph cohesion and, 79
sentence construction and,
66-67
Reports
focus of, 127
formal, 123-127
informal, 120
progress, 121-123
recommendation, 128-129
Responsibility avoidance, dictation and, 105-106

Resumés, 139-140
Robert's Rules of Order, 94-95
Rockefeller, Sr., John D., 160
Run-on sentences, 68

Sales force, memo used with, 115
Sales letters, 133, 134-137
    closings of, 46
    repetition in, 66-67
Salutation, 33-34
    see also Letters, opening of
Selectric typewriter, 155
Semicolon, 67-70
Sentence
    construction, 28, 66-67
    compound, 69, 74
    length, 51
    run-on, 68
    simple, 74
    topic, 76-78
Sex, determining from letter, 34
Sexist language, 13, 83-85
    government and, 84, 93, 96
    grammar and, 91-93
    guidelines for avoiding, 85-88
    job titles, 96-97
    males affected by, 93-94
    Mr., Mrs., Ms. and, 95-96
    salutation, 33
    stereotyping, 88-91
    use of "chair," 94-95
    use of "person," 94-95
Shorthand, 104
    see also Dictation
Simon, Gerald A., 92
Simplification, 8-9, 28-29, 60-61
    attempts at, 10
    formal reports and, 125-126
    of sentences, 74
    word usage and, 50-51
Simplified Form, of salutation, 34
"Sincerely," use of in closings, 47
Slang, 65
Speech habits, *see* Dictation
Split infinitives, 63-64
Staff, costs of, 9-10
Stamps, cost of, 9
    see also Mail
Stand-alone word processors, 156
Stationery, cost of, 9,152-153,
    160-161
Stereotyping, avoiding, 88-91
    see also Sexist language
Stevenson, Robert Louis, 25-26,
    132

Style
    conciseness, 28
    saying what you mean, 26-27
    sentence structure, 28
    simplicity, 28-29
    use of you, 25
    words as you, 25-26
Syllables, counts of, 51
Synonyms, 54-55, 79

Table of Contents
    for formal report, 123
    of proposal, 130-131
Talking mannerisms, *see*
    Dictation
Telephone, word processing
    and, 156
"That," use of, 58-59
Timing, of letter 23-24
Titles, sexist language and,
    95-97
Tone, setting the, 35-37
Topic sentence, 35-38
    support of, 76-78
Transitions, paragraph cohesion
    and, 79-80
Transmittal letter, 123
Twain, Mark, 40, 58, 124
Typewriter
    automatic, 153-154
    Selectric, 155

Underlining, 67
Usage, 56
    see also Grammar

Verbs, 56-58, 105

"We," use of, 39-40, 105
"Which," use of, 58-59
Women's liberation, *see* Sexist
    language
Word processors, 154-157
Word usage, 43, 49
    meanings of, 25-26
    misuse, 51-54
    overeducation and, 55
    pronouns, 39-40
    redundancy, 51
    sentence length, 51
    simplicity, 50-51
    syllable counts, 50-51
    synonyms, 54-55
    usage, 56

words as you, 25-26
see also Grammar

You Approach
in application letters, 141
closing of a letter, 46

confirmation purposes and, 39
good will and, 39
opening of a letter, 37-39
in sales letters, 135
"You," use of in dictation, 105